The Stone Age

Titles in the World History Series

The Age of Augustus
The Age of Feudalism
The Age of Pericles
The Alamo
America in the 1960s
The American Frontier
The American Revolution
Ancient Greece
The Ancient Near East
Architecture
Aztec Civilization
The Battle of the
  Little Bighorn
The Black Death
The Byzantine Empire
Caesar's Conquest of Gaul
The California Gold Rush
The Chinese Cultural
  Revolution
The Civil Rights Movement
The Collapse of the
  Roman Republic
The Conquest of Mexico
The Crimean War
The Crusades
The Cuban Missile Crisis
The Cuban Revolution
The Early Middle Ages
Egypt of the Pharaohs
Elizabethan England
The End of the Cold War
The French and Indian War
The French Revolution
The Glorious Revolution
The Great Depression
Greek and Roman
  Mythology
Greek and Roman Science

Greek and Roman Theater
The History of Slavery
Hitler's Reich
The Hundred Years' War
The Industrial Revolution
The Inquisition
The Italian Renaissance
The Late Middle Ages
The Lewis and Clark
  Expedition
The Mexican Revolution
The Mexican War of
  Independence
Modern Japan
The Mongol Empire
The Persian Empire
The Punic Wars
The Reformation
The Relocation of the
  North American Indian
The Renaissance
The Roaring Twenties
The Roman Empire
The Roman Republic
Roosevelt and the New Deal
The Russian Revolution
Russia of the Tsars
The Scientific Revolution
The Spread of Islam
The Stone Age
Traditional Africa
Traditional Japan
The Travels of Marco Polo
Twentieth Century Science
The Wars of the Roses
The Watts Riot
Women's Suffrage

WORLD HISTORY SERIES ■ ■ ■

The Stone Age

by
Patricia D. Netzley

Lucent Books, P.O. Box 289011, San Diego, CA 92198-9011

With appreciation for the Faber family,
and for Raymond, Matthew, Sarah, and Jacob Netzley,
whose love and support I treasure

Library of Congress Cataloging-in-Publication Data

Netzley, Patricia D.
    The Stone Age / by Patricia D. Netzley.
        p. cm. — (The world history series)
    Includes bibliographical references and index.
    Summary: Discusses the long period of human history
known as the Stone Age during which humans evolved into beings capable of inventing and using increasingly sophisticated
tools and creating complex social groupings.
    ISBN 1-56006-316-5 (alk. paper)
    1. Stone age—Juvenile literature. 2. Prehistoric peoples—
Juvenile literature. 3. Human evolution—Juvenile literature.
[1. Stone age. 2. Prehistoric peoples. 3. Human evolution.]
I. Title. II. Series.
GN768.N47   1998
930.1'2—dc21   97-33613
                                                                    CIP
                                                                    AC

Contents

Foreword

Each year on the first day of school, nearly every history teacher faces the task of explaining why his or her students should study history. One logical answer to this question is that exploring what happened in our past explains how the things we often take for granted—our customs, ideas, and institutions—came to be. As statesman and historian Winston Churchill put it, "Every nation or group of nations has its own tale to tell. Knowledge of the trials and struggles is necessary to all who would comprehend the problems, perils, challenges, and opportunities which confront us today." Thus, a study of history puts modern ideas and institutions in perspective. For example, though the founders of the United States were talented and creative thinkers, they clearly did not invent the concept of democracy. Instead, they adapted some democratic ideas that had originated in ancient Greece and with which the Romans, the British, and others had experimented. An exploration of these cultures, then, reveals their very real connection to us through institutions that continue to shape our daily lives.

Another reason often given for studying history is the idea that lessons exist in the past from which contemporary societies can benefit and learn. This idea, although controversial, has always been an intriguing one for historians. Those who agree that society can benefit from the past often quote philosopher George Santayana's famous statement, "Those who cannot remember the past are condemned to repeat it." Historians who ascribe to Santayana's philosophy believe that, for example, studying the events that led up to the major world wars or other significant historical events would allow society to chart a different and more favorable course in the future.

Just as difficult as convincing students to realize the importance of studying history is the search for useful and interesting supplementary materials that present historical events in a context that can be easily understood. The volumes in Lucent Books' World History Series attempt to present a broad, balanced, and penetrating view of the march of history. Ancient Egypt's important wars and rulers, for example, are presented against the rich and colorful backdrop of Egyptian religious, social, and cultural developments. The series engages the reader by enhancing historical events with these cultural contexts. For example, in *Ancient Greece*, the text covers the role of women in that society. Slavery is discussed in *The Roman Empire*, as well as how slaves earned their freedom. The numerous and varied aspects of everyday life in these and other societies are explored in each volume of the series. Additionally, the series covers the major political, cultural, and philosophical ideas as the torch of civilization is passed from ancient Mesopotamia and Egypt, through Greece, Rome, Medieval Europe, and other world cultures, to the modern day.

The material in the series is formatted in a thorough, precise, and organized manner. Each volume offers the reader a comprehensive and clearly written overview of an important historical event or period. The topic under discussion is placed in a broad historical context. For example, *The Italian Renaissance* begins with a discussion of the High Middle Ages and the loss of central control that allowed certain Italian cities to develop artistically. The book ends by looking forward to the Reformation and interpreting the societal changes that grew out of the Renaissance. Thus, students are not only involved in an historical era, but also enveloped by the events leading up to that era and the events following it.

One important and unique feature in the World History Series is the primary and secondary source quotations that richly supplement each volume. These quotes are useful in a number of ways. First, they allow students access to sources they would not normally be exposed to because of the difficulty and obscurity of the original source. The quotations range from interesting anecdotes to farsighted cultural perspectives and are drawn from historical witnesses both past and present. Second, the quotes demonstrate how and where historians themselves derive their information on the past as they strive to reach a consensus on historical events. Lastly, all of the quotes are footnoted, familiarizing students with the citation process and allowing them to verify quotes and/or look up the original source if the quote piques their interest.

Finally, the books in the World History Series provide a detailed launching point for further research. Each book contains a bibliography specifically geared toward student research. A second, annotated bibliography introduces students to all the sources the author consulted when compiling the book. A chronology of important dates gives students an overview, at a glance, of the topic covered. Where applicable, a glossary of terms is included.

In short, the series is designed not only to acquaint readers with the basics of history, but also to make them aware that their lives are a part of an ongoing human saga. Perhaps they will then come to the same realization as famed historian Arnold Toynbee. In his monumental work, *A Study of History*, he wrote about becoming aware of history flowing through him in a mighty current, and of his own life "welling like a wave in the flow of this vast tide."

Important Dates in the History of the Stone Age

ca. 4 million years ago
Australopithecus appeared on Earth.

ca. 2.5 million years ago
Early Stone Age began.

ca. 2 million years ago
Homo habilis appeared.

ca. 1.8 million years ago
Homo erectus appeared.

ca. 1.8 to 1.7 million years ago
Homo habilis disappeared.

ca. 1 million to 700,000 years ago
Australopithecus disappeared.

ca. 500,000 years ago
Homo sapiens appeared.

ca. 200,000–50,000 years ago
Homo sapiens sapiens appeared in Africa.

ca. 130,000 years ago
Neandertals appeared.

ca. 125,000–32,000 years ago
Middle Stone Age.

ca. 100,000 years ago
Homo sapiens sapiens appeared in the Middle East.

ca. 60,000 years ago
Homo sapiens sapiens appeared in Australia.

ca. 50,000–35,000 years ago
Neandertals disappeared.

ca. 32,000–10,000 years ago
Late Stone Age.

ca. 20,000 years ago
Homo sapiens sapiens appeared in Europe.

A.D. 1819
Christian Jurgensen Thomsen creates the historical classifications of Stone Age, Bronze Age, and Iron Age.

1836
Discovery of the first Acheulean stone tools.

1856
Discovery of the first Neandertal fossils.

1859
Publication of Charles Darwin's *On the Origin of Species.*

1871
Publication of Charles Darwin's *The Descent of Man.*

1879
Discovery of Altamira Cave, with Cro-Magnon art, in Spain.

1887
Eugene Dubois finds the first *Homo erectus* fossils, known as Java Man.

1907
Discovery of the first *Homo heidelbergensis* fossils.

1912
Piltdown Man presented to scientific community.

1924
Raymond Dart discovers the first *Australopithecus* fossil, known as the Taung child.

1927–1937
Fossils of the *Homo erectus* known as Peking Man found in China.

1931
Louis and Mary Leakey find the first Oldowan tools at Olduvai Gorge in Africa.

1933
Steinheim fossil (a *Homo sapiens*) found in Germany.

1940
Lascaux Cave, with Cro-Magnon art, discovered in France.

1949
Homo erectus fossils found in Africa.

1953
Piltdown Man determined to be a fake.

1960
At Olduvai Gorge, the Leakeys find the first *Homo habilis* fossil.

1974
"Lucy"—a nearly complete *Australopithecus* skeleton—is discovered.

1994
The Chauvet Cave, with Cro-Magnon art, is discovered in France. 800,000–900,000-year-old bone fragments are found in Ceprano, Italy; research into whether they are *Homo erectus* or *Homo sapiens* continues.

1995
Discovery of 400,000-year-old throwing spears in Schoningen, Germany.

1997
Scientists extract DNA from Neandertal bones discovered in 1856.

The First Humans

Approximately 7 million years ago, the earliest known creatures resembling present-day humans first walked the earth. They were small and apelike, and their ancestors had lived in the branches of African trees. Many scientists now believe that changes in climate triggered the emergence of this different form of ape.

Prehistoric times were marked by several ice ages, when glaciers reached far beyond today's comparatively small north and south polar ice caps. According to science writer Robert Lee Hotz, each of these ice ages seems to have coincided with "the demise [vanishing] of some pre-human species and the development of those who

An illustration depicts how a Stone Age family living a million years ago might have used tools made of bone and horn.

The Science of Archaeology

Because the Stone Age occurred at a time when humans did not have the skills or tools to create written records of their lives, modern people must rely on archaeologists to give them insight into this prehistoric period. Archaeology is a complicated science, as Brian Fagan points out in his book In the Beginning.

"Studying archaeology is one of the primary ways in which humanity's featureless past can be put into . . . perspective. Yet the researches of archaeologists remain surprisingly unfamiliar to the public, which pictures the archaeologist as a gray-bearded treasure hunter, perpetually digging around pyramids. Nothing could be further from the truth. Archaeological research has become meticulous, laborious, and complicated, with many startling achievements to its credit. . . . Major changes in human culture have been traced through millennia of prehistoric times, while increasingly accurate methods of dating the past have been developed and applied to archaeological sites all over the world. The archaeologist's work is transforming featureless prehistory into a fascinating landscape of hominid evolution, cultural change, and technological development—reflecting increased human control over the natural environment. The first steps toward a world prehistory have been taken, giving new perspectives of time and human history, as well as exciting theoretical models of our past."

An archaeology student brushes dirt from the tooth of a giant extinct wolf.

became the forebears of modern humanity."[1] Why should this be? How might changes in global temperature cause some species to become extinct—that is, to disappear—during prehistoric times, and others to appear?

Anthropologist Elisabeth Vrba explains that the increase in glaciation caused global cooling, which means that "the oceans became about five to ten degrees cooler, [and] the average temperature of the globe became considerably cooler."[2] This worldwide drop in temperature affected earth's vegetation. On the continent of Africa, for example, the climate change caused serious reductions in warm, wet, heavily forested areas—the type of habitat favored by tree dwellers.

As the number of trees decreased, it became more difficult for apelike species to find inhabitable branches. Moreover, crowded branches meant more competition for food. Fights broke out over the limited supply of leaves and fruit, and strong creatures drove away weaker ones. Anthropologists Charles Hockett and Robert Ascher explain:

> Population pressure within a diminishing grove would force bands into competition over its resources, and the less powerful bands would be displaced. Also, when a migrating band managed to reach another grove, it would often happen that the new grove was already occupied, and once again there would be competition. Thus, in the long run, the trees would be held by the most powerful, while the less powerful would repeatedly have to get along as best they could in the fringes of the forest or in open country.[3]

Forced out of the trees, these creatures found life difficult. Their long arms, highly effective when swinging from branch to branch, were inefficient on the ground. Their teeth, designed primarily for eating soft fruit and insects, proved ill suited for the harder roots and tubers of the open savanna. Then certain members of the species were born with shorter arms and stronger teeth. These individuals had a better chance of survival because their bodies were better suited to their environment. As they thrived, their favorable physical attributes were passed on to their offspring, and eventually all the members of their species shared one appearance.

Bipedalism

The process whereby a species adapts to changing circumstances in its environment is called *evolution*. Not all species evolve; some fail to adapt and eventually die out. But when evolution does occur, it is an extremely slow process. Many generations must pass before all members of a population exhibit an advantageous evolutionary characteristic.

Moreover, evolutionary changes can be behavioral as well as physical. For example, the most important adaptation in early humans, the switch to *bipedalism*, or walking on two legs, has both components. The behavioral adaptation was the act of walking like a person. The physical adaptation was a collection of features that supported this behavior. For example, changes in arm length, foot structure, and overall body shape, as well as the absence of a tail, encouraged an upright stance.

Scientists consider bipedalism to be the defining feature of creatures who belong to the human, or Hominidae, family.

It was a beneficial adaptation for hominids. Bipedalism not only enabled them to travel longer distances on land, but it helped them stay cool in the hot savanna sun. According to Rod Caird's book *Ape Man: The Story of Human Evolution*:

> Peter Wheeler, an evolutionary biologist . . . who has made a special study of heat loss and retention, argues for a key positive advantage of standing upright. In hot conditions, especially when the sun is fully up, less of the body is exposed to direct sunlight, and accumulated heat in the body can be lost more quickly without consuming large quantities of water. Further, Wheeler thinks that two-legged locomotion, at least at low walking speeds, is less demanding of energy than its four-legged equivalent.[4]

Stone Tools

Although the early hominids walked upright, they were still extremely apelike. In fact, some anthropologists do not call them hominids at all, and scientists have used the Latin name *Australopithecus*, which means "southern ape," to identify their class or genus.

Australopithecines had small brains, and many scientists think they did not know how to hunt or use tools. In addition, their throats were not developed enough for speech. But approximately 2 to 3 million years ago, a new kind of hominid appeared alongside the australopithecine that probably did have these traits. Scientists identified its genus as *Homo*, or "humanlike," and its species as *habilis*, which means "handy or skillful."

Homo habilis had a larger brain than the *Australopithecus*, and some scientists believe it was capable of a rudimentary form of spoken language. Some also believe that it knew how to hunt, as opposed to simply scavenging meat left over from larger carnivores' kills. There is disagreement, however, about how sophisticated this hunting might have been. Some think it is possible that *Homo habilis* hunted large antelopes and similar animals, whereas others consider *habilis* capable of catching and killing only smaller, weaker creatures.

Australopithecus africanus *was able to walk upright, freeing his arms for other activities and allowing him to travel greater distances.*

Scientists Disagree

Scientists have always disagreed about how evidence of Stone Age life should be interpreted. Ian Tattersall suggests that this is partly because scientific opinion is influenced by society. In his book The Fossil Trail, *he says:*

"The starting point for any new set of hypotheses is the set of hypotheses that preceded it; and what we believe today can never be fully independent of what we believed yesterday. Moreover, in anything as close to our own ego as the story of our own origins, what we think we know cannot be independent of what we believe about ourselves. Clearly, it is too much to ask that scientific opinions in this emotive realm should be entirely independent of prevailing social thought and attitudes."

But regardless of their source, meat and other animal parts were a significant part of the *habilis* diet, and their protein helped the *habilis* brain grow even larger. Rod Caird explains that "meat and other animal foods like bone marrow are highly nutritious, and the growth of the brain demands substantial quantities of high-quality, readily digestible foods."[5]

With this increase in brain size, as well as the improved movement from bipedalism, came the ability to use tools. Many scientists believe that *Homo habilis* was the first form of human being to use hand axes and other sharpened stone implements, called *flakes*, both to kill and butcher animals and to dig up plants. The appearance of these tools gave the historical period known as the Stone Age its name.

Conditions during the Stone Age will always be a matter of dispute. It is a time without written records, and although scientists have discovered some of the remains of people who lived during the period, they disagree on how these remains should be interpreted. Perhaps one day new evidence and new technologies will lead to a consensus of what Stone Age life was like. In the meantime, learning about evolutionary science inspires people to think about where human beings might have come from, and where they might be going.

1 Classifying Prehistory

The term *Stone Age* was first used by the ancient Romans and Chinese. These early historians studied the tools and materials of previous cultures as a basis for criticizing contemporary life. In her book *The Practical Archaeologist*, Jane McIntosh explains:

> Philosophers such as the Roman Lucretius (96–55 BC) and Yuan K'ang, who lived in China during the 1st century AD, drew upon some remembrance of their ancestors when they wrote about former technological epochs—the age of stone, the age of jade, the age of bronze—and contrasted those with what they saw as the degenerate age of iron in which they themselves were living.[6]

It was not until the early nineteenth century, however, that scholars made specific attempts to apply the approach to archaeological materials. In 1819 the first curator of the Danish National Museum, Christian Jurgensen Thomsen, was reorganizing his museum's artifacts when he decided to display them according to the materials commonly used at their time of manufacture. An *artifact* is any object found at an archaeological site that offers evidence of human activity, such as tools, weapons, and pots. Thomsen divided the museum's artifacts into three sections: the Stone Age, the Bronze Age, and the Iron Age.

In his book *Missing Links: The Hunt for Earliest Man*, John Reader explains the significance of this system:

> Thomsen's three-age system appeared in print in 1836 . . . and spread gradually through Europe to become the fundamental system of classification of prehistoric man. Stone Age, Bronze Age, Iron Age: a chronological succession of increasing sophistication and, it implied, improvement. [However,] by the 1860s . . . it was clear that the term Stone Age was too narrow a classification for all the numerous and varied stone artefacts [*sic*] that archaeologists were discovering, particularly in France.[7]

Dividing the Stone Age

Stone artifacts fell into two distinct types: crudely chipped and highly polished. Therefore archaeologists decided to divide the Stone Age into two halves according to stone technology—the Old Stone Age, or Paleolithic Period, and the New Stone Age, or Neolithic Period.

The terms *Paleolithic* and *Neolithic* were first proposed by a British archaeologist, Sir John Lubbock, in 1865. According to John

Reader, Lubbock defined the Paleolithic Period as a time "when man shared the possession of Europe with [animals like] the Mammoth, the Cave Bear, the Woolly-haired rhinoceros, and other extinct animals" and the Neolithic Period as "the later or polished stone age; a period characterized by beautiful weapons and instruments of flint and other kinds of stone."[8]

The Paleolithic Period stretched from the last part of the Pliocene Epoch, approximately 2.5 million years ago, through the Pleistocene Epoch, which ended 10,000 years ago. Because this period is so long, scientists have further divided it into three parts: the Lower, or Early, Paleolithic Period, which ended approximately 125,000 years ago; the Middle, or Mousterian, Paleolithic Period, which ended approximately 32,000 years ago; and the Upper, or Late, Paleolithic Period, which ended approximately 10,000 years ago. Again, scientists used subtle differences in tool technology to establish these divisions.

The Neolithic Period, which began approximately 10,000 years ago, lasted until the beginning of the Bronze Age, which occurred at various times in various places. In many parts of the Near East, for example, the Bronze Age began around 3000 B.C., whereas there is no evidence that bronze was used in China before 1600 B.C. The Neolithic Period marks the beginning of agriculture, animal husbandry, and pottery manufacture; its tools reflect these new activities.

The Stone Age continued to be divided into two periods, the Paleolithic and the Neolithic, until the 1950s, when new discoveries prompted archaeologist V. Gordon Childe to identify a third period. Called the Middle Stone Age, or Mesolithic Period, it began in approximately 8300 B.C.

A Neolithic whetstone has been shaped by an early Stone Age hominid for use in polishing flint or bone implements.

and lasted until approximately 6000 B.C. However, it occurred only in northwestern Europe, where the harsher climate resulted in tools and behavior that differed from those typical of warmer regions.

Geological Classifications

All three periods of the Stone Age took place at a time in the earth's geologic history called the Cenozoic Era. The Cenozoic Era was one of several eras, or divisions of time, that have been identified by geologists studying layers, or strata, of rock and soil. One way to estimate the passage of time in periods (before there were people able to make calendars or keep permanent records) is to measure changes in the earth's stratification, or layered makeup.

In his book *In the Beginning*, Brian Fagan explains the concept behind this branch of geology, which is called *stratigraphy*.

> If I place a book on the table, and then pile another one on top of it, clearly the upper one of the two was placed on the table after, and at a later moment in time than, the original volume. The second book became part of the pile after the first—though how long afterward we have no means of telling. This example illustrates [the concept behind stratigraphy]. . . .
>
> The basic principle in most stratigraphic observation is a simple one: the geological layers of the earth are superimposed on one another almost like the layers of a cake. Easily viewed examples are cliffs by the seashore or in quarries that show a series of geological levels. . . . The superposition of a series of occupation levels or geological strata in order can be achieved by many different processes; wind erosion, water action, earthquakes, and glacial action have all played their part in the accumulation of the earth's strata.[9]

Different geological time periods are tagged on a dirt cliff at an archaeological site in Wyoming. Identifying layers allows archaeologists to roughly date their findings.

It was a nineteenth-century geologist, Sir Charles Lyell, who introduced the use of stratification to determine time periods. He divided geologic history into four eras on the basis of major geographical events, such as glacial action. His classification system was published and expanded during the 1830s, and in 1841 English geologist John Phillips used it to identify the Cenozoic Era, which scientists have also called "The Age of Mammals."

The Cenozoic Era stretched from 65 million years ago to the present, and geologists have divided it into two periods. In Europe these periods are called the Paleogene and the Neogene, but elsewhere the terms *Tertiary* and *Quaternary* are preferred. The Tertiary Period began approximately 65 million years ago, whereas the Quaternary Period began approximately 1.8 million years ago and continues to the present.

Geologists further divide these periods into epochs. In his book *The Human Career: Human Biological and Cultural Origins*, Richard Klein gives the following rough breakdown. The Tertiary Period has five epochs: the Paleocene Epoch (lasting from 65 to 54 million years ago), the Eocene Epoch (54 to 38 million years ago), the

Oligocene Epoch (38 to 23 million years ago), the Miocene Epoch (23 to 5.5 million years ago), and the Pliocene Epoch (5.5 to 1.7 million years ago), when the earliest hominids appeared. The Quaternary Period has been divided into the Pleistocene Epoch (lasting from 1.7 million years ago to 10,000 years ago) and the Holocene Epoch (10,000 years ago to the present).

Ignoring Evidence

Most of the Stone Age took place during the Pleistocene Epoch. However, the epoch was identified long before scientists became convinced that early humans lived during that time. This was partly because some of the most important evidence of prehistoric life was either lost or ignored. For example, prehistoric human skull fragments discovered in Germany in 1700 were set aside in a museum and forgotten until scientists began to examine them 135 years later. Tattersall says that another skull "found in Gibraltar during work on military fortifications in 1848 or earlier . . . also sat neglected on a shelf for many years before its importance became understood."[10]

But even when evidence of prehistoric life was present it was often misunderstood, because most people could not imagine human beings using objects so different from their own. For example, from ancient Roman times until the 1600s, people invented strange reasons for the existence of prehistoric stone tools. Ian Tattersall, in *The Fossil Trail*, says:

Flaked flint tools, known in Europe from time immemorial, were acknowledged to be curiosities that required explanation. Such explanations were as varied as they were imaginative: petrified thunderbolts, fairy arrows, exhalations of the clouds.[11]

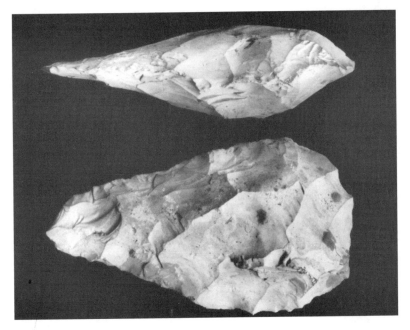

Quartz implements dating from the Stone Age have sharpened edges. Early Romans, trying to explain such tools, identified them as petrified thunderbolts and other unlikely items.

But in the 1600s, a few scholars suggested that these ancient items might somehow be related to human activity. For example, in 1655, Isaac de la Peyrere of Bordeaux, France, speculated in print that such objects might have belonged to ancient people who predated the first man mentioned in the Bible. His words immediately got him into trouble.

At the time, most people believed in the absolute, literal truth of the Bible, which says that God created the first people, Adam and Eve, at the very beginning of time. Some editions of the King James Bible even offered the date of Creation: 4004 B.C. This date was developed by a religious scholar, an Irish archbishop named James Ussher, who used time references in the Bible to construct a system of biblical chronology. Ussher's system was widely accepted by religious leaders. Therefore, when de la Peyrere offered a different view, the Roman Catholic Church accused him of heresy, which meant he was an enemy of the church. French officials then threw him in jail and burned his book.

By the eighteenth century, this type of persecution had eased. Nonetheless, most people continued to believe that prehistoric artifacts were no older than 4004 B.C. As Jane McIntosh describes in her book *The Practical Archaeologist,*

> The upsurge of interest in [looking for artifacts] in 18th-century Europe revealed more and more remains of unfamiliar beasts, birds, fish and plants, often deep in the ground. The orthodox explanation was that the creatures and plants had been destroyed by [the biblical event of] Noah's flood—thus reconciling them with the Bible. People who believed it came to be called "cata-strophists," or "diluvianists," the latter from *dilivium,* the Latin word for flood.[12]

Moreover, although they were no longer thrown in jail for believing otherwise, people who suggested that human beings predated the Bible continued to be ridiculed or called atheists. For example, James Hutton, considered the founder of modern geology, was severely criticized for his suggestion that the earth was actually billions of years old.

Hutton based this hypothesis on a study of rock erosion, which is a slow process. As McIntosh explains,

> Hutton observed the natural processes that form and shape the landscape, and maintained that these processes had occurred in exactly the same way throughout the past and that they would continue to do so in the future. "We find no vestige of a beginning, no prospect of an end (in nature)," he wrote.[13]

A New Theory

Despite opposition from catastrophists, Hutton gained followers, and gradually his ideas came to be accepted by more and more scientists. One of the most important of these was British naturalist Charles Darwin. In 1859 Darwin published a book called *On the Origin of Species* (often called by the mistaken, and misleading, title *The Origin of the Species*), in which he suggested that one type of creature might gradually, over many generations, develop into another. This idea was called the "theory of evolution."

Darwin was not the first to publish a book on the subject of evolution. Fifteen

Difficult Conditions

Early archaeologists and paleontologists often worked under difficult conditions. Moreover, according to John Reader, few people were interested in hearing about their discoveries or visiting their sites. In Missing Links: The Hunt for Earliest Man, *Reader quotes from Sir Charles Lyell's 1863 book* The Antiquity of Man *to illustrate the problems of one of the first paleontologists, Paul Schmerling, who excavated the Engis caves in Belgium during the early 1800s.*

"To be let down, as Schmerling was, day after day, by a rope tied to a tree so as to slide to the foot of the first opening of the Engis cave, where the best-preserved human skulls were found; and, after thus gaining access to the first subterranean gallery, to creep on all fours through a contracted passage leading to larger chambers, there to superintend by torchlight, week after week and year after year, the workmen who were breaking through the stalagmite underlaying bone breccia nearly as hard; to stand for hours with one's feet in the mud and with water dripping from the roof on one's head, in order to mark the position and guard against the loss of each single bone of a skeleton, and at length after finding leisure, strength and courage for all these operations, to look forward, as the fruits of one's labour, to the publication of unwelcome intelligence, opposed to the prepossessions [preconceptions] of the scientific and as well as the unscientific public—when these circumstances are taken into account, we need scarcely wonder, not only that a passing traveller failed to stop and scrutinise the evidence, but that a quarter of a century should have elapsed before even the neighbouring professors of the University of Liege came forth to vindicate the truthfulness of their indefatigable [tireless] and clear-sighted countryman."

years earlier, a science journalist named Robert Chambers introduced evolutionary theory in his *Vestiges of the Natural History of Creation.* However, Chambers's book, according to Darwin himself, contained "little accurate knowledge and a great want of scientific caution,"[14] whereas Darwin's *Origin of Species* was carefully wrought. Therefore, Darwin's work was taken more seriously.

Because it led some readers to speculate that human beings might also have evolved from another species, *Origin of Species* was extremely controversial, as was Darwin's 1871 book, *The Descent of Man*, in which he contended that humans and apes had a common ancestor. By the time *The Descent of Man* was published, other scientists besides Darwin had already proposed this idea. Many of them had begun

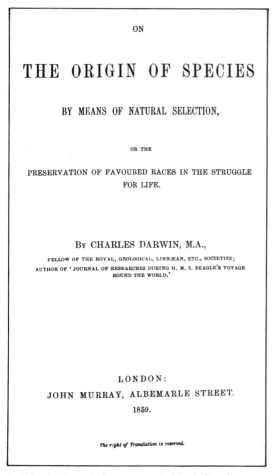

ON

THE ORIGIN OF SPECIES

BY MEANS OF NATURAL SELECTION,

OR THE

PRESERVATION OF FAVOURED RACES IN THE STRUGGLE
FOR LIFE.

By CHARLES DARWIN, M.A.,

FELLOW OF THE ROYAL, GEOLOGICAL, LINNÆAN, ETC., SOCIETIES;
AUTHOR OF 'JOURNAL OF RESEARCHES DURING H. M. S. BEAGLE'S VOYAGE
ROUND THE WORLD.'

LONDON:
JOHN MURRAY, ALBEMARLE STREET.
1859.

The right of Translation is reserved.

In Charles Darwin's controversial book On the Origin of Species, *he postulated that modern animals may have evolved from less complex forms.*

to search for evidence of this common ancestor—a creature that was half human, half primate—which they referred to as the "Missing Link." John Reader explains:

> The theory of evolution . . . implied that man was simply a product of life on earth, not its ultimate purpose; it suggested that his origins were shared by the animals of the jungle. An outrageous idea. But if it were true, then the proof would be found in the . . . remains of early man, which would link

man to an earlier form. And since the theory of evolution proposed that man and the apes shared a common ancestor, then the link could be expected to bear some attributes of both. So began the search for the "Missing Link," keenly followed by evolutionist and anti-evolutionist alike—the former seeking the incontrovertible evidence that would establish the theory as fact, the latter anxious to prove that the link was indeed missing, thus reconfirming the belief that the human form had remained unchanged since the day of creation.[15]

No evidence of this Missing Link has ever been found, and today some people suspect that evolution is too gradual and too complicated a process for such a creature to have existed. Others believe that evolution is not gradual at all. In 1972 American paleontologist and evolutionary biologist Stephen Jay Gould proposed that a species remains unchanged for millions of years and that this period of inactivity is followed by a burst of spontaneous evolution. Gould therefore believes that Darwin's theory of evolution is flawed.

Many of Darwin's contemporaries in the scientific community believed his theory was completely wrong. One of his most vocal opponents was British anatomist and paleontologist Richard Owen, who rejected the idea that humans evolved from apes. According to John Reader,

> In 1855, Owen used his anatomical expertise in an attempt to disprove the theory of evolution at its most controversial point—man's link with the apes. The occasion was an evening meeting of the Royal Institution of Great Britain. . . . Beginning and ending with

disparaging remarks on those who supported the evolutionary theory, Owen endeavored to show that although ape and man are structurally very similar, the differences between them are much more relevant. He mentioned especially the differences that are not subject to external influences, and therefore should be passed from generation to generation without modification, appearing exactly alike in ancestor and descendant. Owen cited the gorilla's prominent eyebrow ridge as an example of such a feature. There is no muscle attached to it, he pointed out, nor is there any aspect of the gorilla's behaviour which suggests that the prominent ridge could be lost or gained by external causes operating on successive generations. Therefore the ridges must have occurred in the gorilla's ancestors, said Owen, and should occur in all that ancestor's descendants. It followed that if man and gorilla shared a common ancestor, they should also share the prominent eyebrow ridge. But ridges rarely—and then only feebly—occur in man, he pointed out; therefore man and gorilla could not have an ancestor in common. Thus, Owen concluded, the notion that man had evolved from the apes was disproved.[16]

Reader finds it ironic that Owen used the example of the eyebrow ridge in his criticism of evolutionary theory because

> the first fossil to be accepted as evidence of early man's physical form, Neanderthal Man . . . presented prominent eyebrow ridges as its most distinctive feature. Since 1857, when the Neanderthal remains were found, the

prominent ridges above its eyes, which Owen claimed were an exclusively ape-like feature, have become symbolic of early man.[17]

Better Methods for Dating Fossils

Bones become fossils only after their organic components have been infiltrated and replaced by minerals. Fossilization is a long, slow process. However, when evidence of Neandertal (formerly Neanderthal) Man was first discovered, scientists did not know how old it was. Since they did not yet have techniques for analyzing the chemical composition of fossils, they had to rely on visual appearance, which could be misleading. As John Reader explains,

> The fossil remains of marine creatures, extinct elephants and so forth are unmistakable. Human fossils, on the other hand, are found only in geologically recent—and therefore comparatively shallow—deposits, where they may easily be confused with historically recent burials.[18]

In fact, the limestone workers who discovered the first Neandertal skeleton in a cave in the Neander Valley near Düsseldorf, Germany, discarded it without realizing its importance. Later, a teacher retrieved the skull and some of the bones and sent them to a scientist for study. Soon these fossils became part of the controversy over the theory of evolution.

As scientists discovered more human fossils, they too became a part of this controversy. But gradually, during the late 1800s and early 1900s, most people came to accept the idea that human beings had not always walked on earth in their present form.

At the same time, scientists began to develop better ways to establish how old a fossil might be. They realized that geological stratification could tell them the approximate age of a fossil, but only if they kept detailed notes regarding that fossil's exact position within the rock layers. Scientists also learned that it was important to study the past uses of archaeological sites. Brian Fagan explains:

> [One] factor that may affect the interpretation of stratigraphy is the breaks or disruptions in the layering caused by human activity. Later occupants of a village may dig rubbish pits or graves into earlier strata. Cattle may be kept on the site, their hooves removing the soil and disturbing the upper levels of the underlying horizons; this process also may be caused by later people cultivating the rich soils of an abandoned village site. Building activities may cause foundation trenches and even stone walls to be sunk into earlier levels. Local inhabitants' technological level has a direct bearing on their ability to destroy evidence of earlier occupation. . . . Burrowing animals, too, enjoy archaeological sites, worming their way through the soft, organic soils of caves or village sites and disrupting stratigraphic observations over large areas of the settlement.[19]

However, according to archaeologist Richard Klein, even with such disruptions, dating a group of fossils found at the same site is still relatively easy.

The Fossilization Process

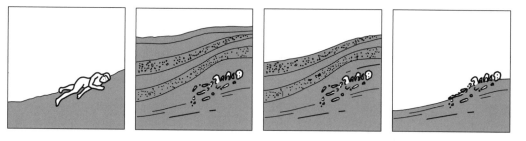

Fossils are the remains of plants and animals preserved in rock. In animals, usually only the hard parts of the body—the teeth and bones—become fossilized. This happens over thousands of years and only when conditions are just right. First, the body must be buried quickly, for example, under ash from a volcanic explosion or mud from a flood. After burial, the body must lie undisturbed for a very long time. Even then, a bone will not become a fossil unless the soil's moisture and chemical content are right.

The transformation from bone to fossil begins when collagen, or protein, leaves the bones and is replaced by minerals from the ground. The minerals turn the bones to stone, making them hard, heavy, and strong. The soil under which the bones are buried also hardens into rock. Under the pressure of layers of rock, the fossils often break into many tiny fragments.

Then, conditions change. The rock begins to split or erode until finally the layer of rock containing the fossil becomes exposed. Eventually, further erosion washes the fossils out of the rock, and they lie exposed on the surface. This is the moment they must be found, before they are trampled by animals or buried in the mud again.

An archaeologist notes the discovery of a Neandertal skull in his journal. Notes detailing the exact location of an archaeological discovery help scientists ascertain the age and function of fossils and artifacts.

All other things being equal, objects found in higher rock layers postdate ones found in deeper layers. The qualification "all other things being equal" is necessary because burrowing animals, invading roots, and the like can displace objects into lower or higher layers, while crustal movements, landslides, and other geomorphic [earth-changing] events can even reverse a stratigraphic sequence, placing older layers on top of younger ones. However, where such disturbances occur, their effects are often minor, detectable, or both, and [this technique] has been fruitfully applied at countless archeological and fossil sites. Its main limitation is that, in the most literal sense, it cannot be used to date objects in layers that do not physically overlap, that is, ones that occur at physically separate sites.[20]

When scientists want to compare fossils from separate sites, they must use their knowledge of the earth's geologic events to help them evaluate the layers in which the fossils were found. In these situations, Klein says, "stratigraphic dating depends on perceived similarities or differences in the properties of two (or more) layers."[21] These properties might involve geologic evidence of changes in climate or ocean levels, or they might involve knowledge about the types of plants found at different rock layers.

Scientists can also use less subjective methods, such as chemical analysis, to determine a fossil's age. For example, they can find out how much of the chemical element fluorine exists in a particular bone and use that information to "date" the object. Klein explains: "Buried bones absorb fluorine from groundwater. Bones that were buried in the same site at the same time should contain the same amount of fluorine."[22] Thus, if tests reveal major differences in fluorine content, the samples probably are of different ages. This method is therefore a comparative one.

To determine the age of an individual fossil, scientists often use radiometric age-dating. This technique analyzes specimens and determines the amount of certain radioactive isotopes within them. An *isotope* is a form of a chemical element that decays, or disintegrates, at a specific constant rate, emitting particles that can be counted. Different elements emit different numbers of particles per second; these rates are known and can be used to determine the age of a fossil.

Unfortunately, radiometric dating cannot be applied to objects older than 40,000 years, since by then their radioactive decay is complete. In other words, there are no

Charles Dawson (holding skull) and other scientists discuss the recently discovered Piltdown skull. Scientists did not discover that the skull was a fraud until forty-one years later.

more particles to be counted. This means that it is impossible to tell whether a specimen is 50,000 or 500,000 years old. Scientists therefore continue to experiment with other ways to pinpoint an older fossil's age.

A Famous Hoax

Of course, such technologies did not exist when the first fossils were discovered. At that time, paleoarchaeologists only had a fossil's position within rock strata as a basis for estimating its age. In fact, their science was so primitive that they had difficulty deciding whether a bone was fossilized, and therefore ancient, or unfossilized, and therefore a recent burial. John Reader reports:

> In the early nineteenth century the "tongue test" was a method commonly used [to determine whether a bone was fossilized or unfossilized], the idea being that bone or fossil adhered to the tongue to a greater or lesser extent depending upon the amount of collagen [a fibrous protein in bone and connective tissue] it contained. However, the tongue test was occasionally contradicted by the hydrochloric acid

test [a chemical technique], which sometimes revealed large quantities of collagen where the tongue test had suggested it was absent.[23]

Because their technology was so primitive, early paleontologists were sometimes the victims of practical jokes. The most famous of these hoaxes involved the "Piltdown Man." The Piltdown Man was first presented to scientists in December 1912 by paleontologist Arthur Smith Woodward, who was in charge of the geology section of the British Museum of Natural History. Woodward had received the fossilized skull pieces from amateur geologist Charles Dawson.

Dawson did not offer much detailed information about his discovery but said that he found the skull pieces over the course of several years, while excavating a gravel pit in the Piltdown Common area of Sussex, England. Reader describes this site:

> The fossil fauna from the pit were of early Pleistocene, or even Pliocene, age, and the flint artefacts [also found there] appeared to be similarly ancient. All of this strongly implied that the human remains found in the same deposit represented the earliest known example of true man.[24]

Nonrenewable Resources

Archaeologists face different challenges than historians face. Not only do archaeologists lack written records to verify their suppositions about the past, but in trying to uncover this information for themselves, they risk destroying it. As Brian Fagan explains in his book In the Beginning,

"The first lesson that any budding excavator learns is that his work is potentially destructive. Excavation is destruction—the archaeological deposits so carefully dissected during any dig are destroyed forever, and their contents removed. . . . There is a radical difference between archaeology and history and other subjects. A scientist can readily recreate the conditions for a basic experiment, the historian can return to his archives for a reevaluation of the complex events in a politician's life. But all that remains after an excavation is the finds from the trenches, the untouched portions of the site, and the photographs, notes, and drawings that record the excavator's observations for posterity. Thus, accurate recording and observation play an overwhelmingly vital role in the day-to-day work of an archaeologist, not only for the sake of the accuracy of his own research, but because he is creating an archive of archaeological information which may be consulted by others. Archaeological sites are nonrenewable resources."

An archaeologist brushes off a condor bone as he works in an excavation site. Archaeologists often risk destroying valuable artifacts while digging through excavation sites.

The Piltdown Man also excited scientists because it had a larger braincase than other early human fossils. This suggested several important new ideas. As Reader explains,

The experts may have . . . argued about the absolute size of the brain, but of one thing they were all certain: the Piltdown remains proved beyond doubt that mankind had already developed a remarkably large brain by the beginning of the Pleistocene. And the implications of this were very important: firstly, a brain so large at that time must have begun its development long before, which implied that true man was very ancient indeed; and second, since the Piltdown remains of this "true man" were older (as it was believed) than the . . . Neanderthal fossils, they firmly dismissed those "brutish" creatures from the line to the status of

"aberrant offshoots," evolutionary experiments that led to extinction—cousins of mankind perhaps, but not ancestors.[25]

However, forty-one years later, scientists discovered that the Piltdown Man was a carefully constructed fake. The new technology of fluorine dating showed that the skull and jaw pieces were of different ages. In fact, the skull pieces were not much older than the hoax itself. Someone had stained the pieces to achieve a fossilized look and had filed down the molar teeth to match the appearance that would have been expected for a prehistoric man.

No one knows who perpetrated this hoax. By the time it was uncovered, the major participants in the fossils' discovery had died. As John Reader points out, however, the incident offers an important lesson for researchers.

Scientists Fooled

In their book Lucy, *Donald Johanson and Maitland Edey describe how the Piltdown hoax fooled many prominent scientists, including British anatomist Sir Arthur Keith, who was considered by many to be an expert at authenticating fossils.*

"Poor Keith. Revelation of the Piltdown hoax had come as a heavy blow to his professional pride. He was in his late eighties and living in retirement when [two people] visited him and broke the news of the hoax. 'It will take me a little while to adjust to the new view,' he had whispered. Whether or not he managed, he never said. He was far from the anthropological scene, in the mists of old age, and died eighteen months later, well before he had a chance to learn that during his entire lifetime of estimating fossil ages he had . . . miscalculated the age of every one."

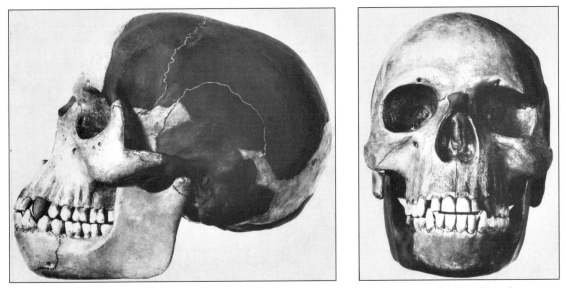

Two views of the infamous Piltdown skull. Fluorine dating methods revealed that the skull and jaw fragments purported to belong to the Piltdown Man were of different ages.

The inconclusive nature of the Piltdown affair reflects a fundamental problem of the science as a whole, for the fossil evidence of human evolution rarely offers just one clear interpretation. At the same time, however, the Piltdown affair makes two pertinent points: first, accurate geological and stratigraphical determinations are essential; and second, when preconception is so clearly defined, so easily reproduced, so enthusiastically welcomed and so long accommodated, as in the case of the Piltdown Man, science reveals a disturbing predisposition towards belief before investigation, as perhaps the hoaxer was anxious to demonstrate.[26]

Scientific procedures are much more accurate today than they were when the Piltdown Man was discovered, but scientists still disagree on some aspects of early human evolution and civilization. They particularly argue about early human behavior. For example, some doubt that early humans could speak very well, while others think they did have this ability. However, most scientists do agree on the basic physical characteristics of early humans, and they are able to identify which types of people lived in each period of the Stone Age.

2 In the Beginning: *Australopithecus* and *Homo Habilis*

Australopithecines first appeared on earth during the Lower Paleolithic Period. These creatures were humanlike apes, and there were several species of them, all members of the genus *Australopithecus*. Some scientists divide this genus into two branches: *Australopithecus robustus*, which became extinct about 1 million years ago, and *Australopithecus gracile*, to which modern humans are related.

All species of *Australopithecus* look slightly different from one another. Some of these differences are so extreme that scientists continue to disagree about whether they should all be classified together. In fact, the species *Australopithecus praegens* (also called *Australopithecus ramidus*), which is more apelike than *Australopithecus*, was recently reclassified as a new, separate genus, *Ardipithecus*.

The Taung Child

The first *Australopithecus* fossil was identified in 1924, when a student brought a fossilized baboon skull to anatomy professor Raymond Dart. The skull came from a lime quarry near Johannesburg, South Africa, in a region called Taung, and Dart decided to investigate the site further. He arranged for the quarry master to send him blocks of rock from the location and immediately found what appeared to be bones from a very young hominid. He assembled the pieces until he had a skull.

Dart called his discovery the "Taung child" and classified it as *Australopithecus africanus*, or "southern ape of Africa." However, many of Dart's contemporaries disagreed with his classification. They criti-

Raymond Dart displays the original Taung specimen of Australopithecus, *which he discovered in 1924.*

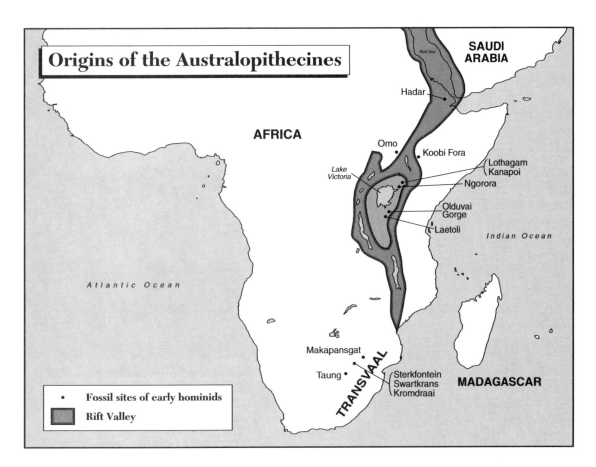

Origins of the Australopithecines

AFRICA

SAUDI ARABIA

Red Sea

Hadar

Omo

Koobi Fora

Lothagam
Kanapoi

Lake Victoria

Ngorora

Olduvai Gorge

Laetoli

Indian Ocean

Atlantic Ocean

Makapansgat

TRANSVAAL

Taung

Sterkfontein
Swartkrans
Kromdraai

MADAGASCAR

• **Fossil sites of early hominids**

■ **Rift Valley**

cized Dart's research methods and, according to modern anthropologist Richard Klein, their criticisms seemed to be justified.

> There were fundamental scientific concerns. . . . There was very little from which to estimate the antiquity of the Taung skull, but some authorities felt that the associated baboon fossils implied it was too recent to be a human ancestor. In addition, the discovery of primitive human fossils ([classified as] "Pithecanthropus") in Java in 1891 had convinced many specialists that Asia, not Africa, was the cradle of humanity. Finally, the skull did not fit either of the current theories of human evolution. . . . The first held that human ancestors

should be equally primitive in all traits, while Dart's find showed a mix of advanced and primitive features. The second theory, supported by the famous Piltdown skull (later exposed as an elaborate fake), proposed that the peculiarly human brain had evolved before other uniquely human traits. The Taung skull, as interpreted by Dart, suggested just the reverse—that the uniquely human mode of bipedal locomotion had evolved before the brain.[27]

In addition, because of the way teeth erupt and brains develop, the skulls of children and apes appear very similar. Therefore many scientists believed that Dart's fossil was actually from an early ape.

One of Dart's few supporters was paleoanthropologist Robert Broom, who decided to look for fossils from an adult *Australopithecus*. In 1936 he found the skull of one in the Transvaal area of South Africa. Two years later, a schoolboy found another hominid fossil near Broom's archaeological site, which led Broom to explore the area further. This resulted in his second *Australopithecus* discovery, which included not only skull fragments but leg bones.

Klein says that these discoveries enabled Broom to "show that adult australopithecines were no more apelike than the Taung child."[28] Moreover, Broom's subsequent writings led "most authorities . . . to accept the australopithecines as hominids, though some were disturbed by Broom's tendency to divide the known fossils into more [categories] than seemed warranted."[29]

Because the first *Australopithecus* that Broom discovered looked slightly different from the Taung child, he classified it as a new genus and species, *Plesianthropus transvaalensis*, or "near man of the Transvaal," rather than as *Australopithecus*. Similarly, he called his second discovery *Paranthropus robustus*, or "next to man and robust." In 1939 scientists decided that both the *Plesianthropus* and the *Paranthropus* were actually different versions of the same species as the Taung child, and they reclassified Broom's discoveries as the *Australopithecus transvaalensis* and *Australopithecus robustus*.

Klein explains that these names are still a matter of some dispute.

Most specialists today place all the fossils in the single genus *Australopithecus*, divisible into two species—*A. africanus* . . . and *A. robustus*. . . . However, a growing number have resurrected the

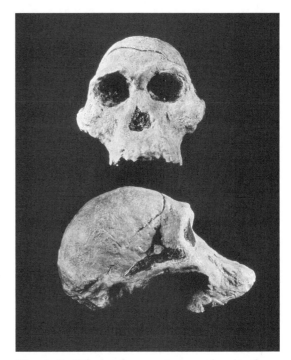

The skull of Plesianthropus transvaalensis, *the first australopithecine fossil discovered by Robert Broom. Broom's discovery was confirmed to be the same species as the Taung child.*

category *Paranthropus* as originally defined by Broom. In the vernacular, *A. africanus* is often called the "gracile (slender) australopithecine" and *A.* (or *Paranthropus*) *robustus* is the "robust australopithecine," although they differed less in the body mass and other features than the names imply.[30]

Lucy

Scientists were able to learn a great deal about australopithecines from Broom's skull and leg fragments. However, from such scant evidence it was difficult to make deductions about how these creatures walked and moved. Scientists needed more

Savage Beasts

People of the early 1900s incorrectly believed that early hominids must have been extremely savage creatures. Even scholars made unsupported statements in this regard. For example, Raymond Dart, who discovered the first Australopithecus *fossil, is quoted in the book* Lucy, *by Donald Johanson and Maitland Edey, as saying:*

"Man's predecessors differed from living apes in being confirmed killers; carnivorous creatures, that seized living quarries by violence, battered them to death, tore apart their broken bodies, dismembered them limb from limb, slaking their ravenous thirst with the hot blood of victims and greedily devouring livid writhing flesh."

An artist's rendition depicts an early hominid emerging from his prehistoric cave. During the early 1900s, many people believed that these creatures were savage beasts.

fossils in order to draw conclusions about the appearance and behavior of the species.

Fortunately, in 1974 a team of American, French, and Ethiopian researchers unearthed an almost complete 3.5-million-year-old female *Australopithecus* skeleton in Ethiopia. It was discovered in a badlands area called Hadar, whose strata had been geologically dated to range from 7 million to 1 million years ago.

The fossils of Lucy (pictured) were discovered in Ethiopia in 1974. Scientists speculate that Lucy is 3.5 million years old.

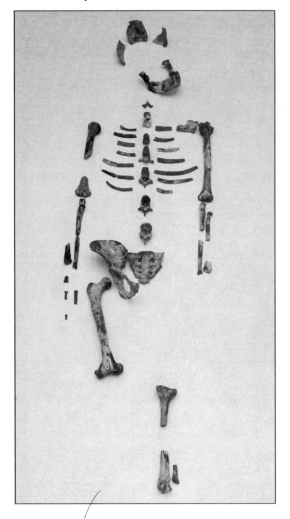

The researchers named their discovery "Lucy." Team member Donald Johanson, the American paleoanthropologist who first spotted fragments of the skeleton, explains the circumstances surrounding her name:

> The camp was rocking with excitement. The first night we never went to bed at all. We talked and talked. . . . There was a tape recorder in the camp, and a tape of the Beatles song "Lucy in the Sky with Diamonds" went belting out into the night sky, and was played at full volume over and over again out of sheer exuberance. At some point during that unforgettable evening—I no longer remember exactly when—the new fossil picked up the name of Lucy, and has been so known ever since, although its proper name—its acquisition number in the Hadar collection—is AL 288-1.[31]

Lucy was a significant discovery because she verified what many people had long suspected about the age of the earliest hominids. By the 1970s, researchers had begun to apply the science of molecular biology, which involves the study of cells, to questions involving human ancestry. Human and animal cells contain a molecule called DNA (deoxyribonucleic acid). DNA carries genetic information and is the basis of heredity, passing copies of itself from one generation to the next. Therefore, by comparing human and chimpanzee DNA, for example, researchers can determine how closely the two species are related.

According to Rod Caird, DNA expert Morris Goodman has determined "that there is only a 1.7 percent difference between chimps and humans, and a 1.9 percent difference between a human and a gorilla, or between a chimp and a gorilla.

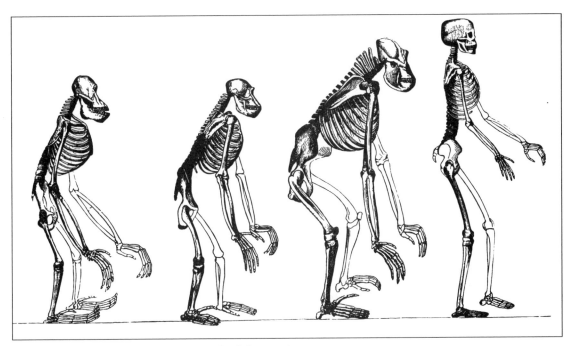

(From left to right) A diagram compares the skeletons of an orangutan, a chimpanzee, and a gorilla to that of a modern human.

The difference between all three and an orang-utan is about 3.7 percent."[32] Caird says that these findings prove that

> the split between orang-utans on the one hand and humans, chimps, and gorillas on the other must have predated the splits between chimps, humans and gorillas. And, most provocatively, it looks as though the split between humans and chimps came later than that between chimps and gorillas.[33]

Goodman has also estimated the approximate date of these splits, using calculations regarding the rate at which certain changes in DNA occur over generations. Based on his research, many scientists concluded that the common ancestor of hominids and chimpanzees lived approximately 5 to 7 million years ago, when the DNA of the two species diverged. The

discovery of Lucy helped support this conclusion. As Rod Caird explains,

> One of the great excitements of the Lucy find was the close dating match with the information provided by molecular research about the common ancestor. The molecular biologists had offered a date of five to seven million years ago for the split between the hominid and chimpanzee lines; here was a bipedal creature, with strong ape-like features as well, dating at three million years ago. The fossil and molecular evidence seemed to be telling the same story.[34]

Moreover, Lucy's body structure confirmed that australopithecines had walked upright on two legs. However, scientists disagree on whether her species had this ability for long. Caird reports:

[Anatomist Owen] Lovejoy believes, from a study of Lucy's leg and foot bones, that by the time she was alive bipedalism had been established for as long as two million years. This was no halfway-house species trying out a new way of getting around with a staggering gait. Lucy and her relatives, according to Lovejoy, were confident and effective on two legs and came from a long line of upright ancestors.[35]

However, other scientists interpret the structure of Lucy's leg and foot bones differently. For example, according to Rod Caird,

Bernard Wood, of Liverpool University, says that Lucy's limb proportions and skeleton suggest she was neither predominantly tree-living nor fully upright, that she and her relatives "may therefore have fed and moved much like modern baboons, but with more emphasis on bipedalism. Such groups would have spread out to forage on the ground in the day, and they congregated, perhaps in caves or trees, at night.". . . [In addition, American paleontologist] Bill Kimbel says the fossil evidence thus far cannot provide all the answers. There is no doubt that Lucy walked upright, but according to Kimbel, whether she was also able to get around in the trees, either to sleep or to avoid predators, can only be speculated about.[36]

But while scientists continue to debate australopithecine behavior, they are certain of their appearance. In size, they ranged from approximately 3 feet 3 inches tall and 66 pounds (females) to 4 feet 11 inches tall and 66 to 154 pounds (largest males). They had short legs and long arms, and their shoulders were slightly hunched. Their hands were very similar to those of modern humans, but their faces somewhat resembled a chimpanzee, with prominent jaws, small skulls, and large canine teeth. Scientists also believe they probably had a light covering of chimpanzee-like hair, not just on their heads but over most of their body as well, because no remains of clothing have ever been found at an *Australopithecus* site.

Some aspects of australopithecine appearance were related to diet. They undoubtedly ate fruit, berries, nuts, and seeds, just as their tree-dwelling ancestors had. But many scientists believe that australopithecines also ate insects, reptiles, eggs, and meat. These new foods quite likely contributed to the differences in facial structure that began to distinguish hominids from apes. Long canine teeth, so well adapted to fibers and the tough skins of tropical vegetables, were less essential for diets that featured a wider variety of foods.

The fossil evidence shows that the jaws and teeth of australopithecines were smaller than the apes of the period. However, those of *Australopithecus robustus* were still extremely large in comparison to modern humans. *Australopithecus gracile* had smaller jaws and smaller molar teeth than *Australopithecus robustus,* and it might have been shorter as well.

Although they ate meat, australopithecines were probably not hunters. They were most likely scavengers, eating whatever other animals left behind. Many scientists believe that australopithecines were unable to hunt because they lacked the intelligence to do so. Their brains were small in relation to their body weight, and fossils suggest that their vocal apparatus was extremely primitive. This means that they were probably unable to communicate with one another by means of speech.

However, it is likely that they communicated well in nonverbal ways, because they lived in family groups. Scientists know this because the year after Lucy's discovery, they began to find more australopithecine skeletons at the same site. In total, fossils from thirteen individuals were recovered. Scientists have named this group the "First Family," and they have speculated about how these creatures died.

It was clear from the way these fossils were found that all the members of the First Family had died at the same time. Scientists therefore ruled out the possibility

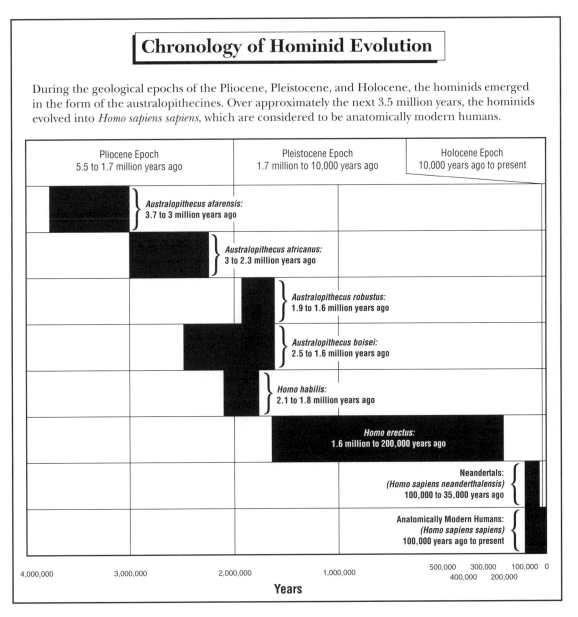

Chronology of Hominid Evolution

During the geological epochs of the Pliocene, Pleistocene, and Holocene, the hominids emerged in the form of the australopithecines. Over approximately the next 3.5 million years, the hominids evolved into *Homo sapiens sapiens*, which are considered to be anatomically modern humans.

Pliocene Epoch	Pleistocene Epoch	Holocene Epoch
5.5 to 1.7 million years ago	1.7 million to 10,000 years ago	10,000 years ago to present

Australopithecus afarensis:
3.7 to 3 million years ago

Australopithecus africanus:
3 to 2.3 million years ago

Australopithecus robustus:
1.9 to 1.6 million years ago

Australopithecus boisei:
2.5 to 1.6 million years ago

Homo habilis:
2.1 to 1.8 million years ago

Homo erectus:
1.6 million to 200,000 years ago

Neandertals:
(Homo sapiens neanderthalensis)
100,000 to 35,000 years ago

Anatomically Modern Humans:
(Homo sapiens sapiens)
100,000 years ago to present

4,000,000   3,000,000   2,000,000   1,000,000   500,000   300,000   100,000   0
                                                      400,000   200,000

Years

of a series of individual accidents or fatal diseases. There was also no sign of violence, so scientists knew the hominid group had not died in a prehistoric war. Nor could the deaths have been due to predators, which would have scattered the bones. In fact, precisely because the bones were not scattered, scientists suspected that the thirteen deaths occurred in a location that was out of the reach of scavengers. Many therefore concluded that the First Family had died in a sudden flood. Although the area of Ethiopia where Lucy was found is dry today, scientists believe that it was once a place of abundant rivers, tall grasslands, and forests. This landscape allowed australopithecines to thrive. According to Caird,

> Common sense and simple arithmetic lead to the conclusion that . . . many hundreds of thousands, probably millions, of Lucy's relatives [once] existed. In an article in the *Cambridge Encyclopedia of Human Evolution* Bernard Wood says that the entire australopithecine fossil collection represents

between 0.02 and 0.00002 percent of the estimated living population of those species.[37]

Olduvai Gorge

Australopithecines shared their environment with another hominid, one that knew how to make and use tools. The first evidence of this was found at a site called the Olduvai Gorge. Located in East Africa on the southeastern Serengeti Plains, the Olduvai Gorge is a steep canyon whose bare sides were worn away by an ancient river. Even before excavating the site, archaeologists Louis and Mary Leakey were certain that the Gorge soil would yield many fossils and artifacts. In fact, John Reader reports that "[Louis] Leakey was so confident that there must be some evidence of Stone Age culture in the Gorge that he bet [another scientist ten British pounds] he would find a stone tool within twenty-four hours of arriving there."[38] Leakey won the bet.

A reconstruction shows how Australopithecus *may have appeared. Scientists believe australopithecines lived in family groups and shared a nonverbal form of communication.*

The Olduvai Gorge in Tanzania has yielded numerous human fossils and artifacts. The first Oldowan tools were discovered at this site by renowned archaeologists Louis and Mary Leakey.

From 1931, when that discovery was made, until today, thousands of stone tools have been found at Olduvai Gorge. The earliest of these were extremely unrefined. In his book *Early Man*, F. Clark Howell says:

> To an untrained person, thinking of the delicately chipped axe and arrowheads made by later and more sophisticated stone cultures, [these] tools might well have appeared to be natural stones. They bore only the faintest resemblance to tools. They were hopelessly crude. Some were large pebbles, others were fist-sized chunks, but all had a few chips struck from one end to make them jagged.[39]

These artifacts are called Oldowan tools, because they were first found in an area of the Olduvai Gorge that archaeologists named the Oldowan Industrial Complex. Similar items from the same period were subsequently found in other sites. All of these tools were made in a similar style,

leading Klein to conclude that Oldowan tools exhibit "remarkable uniformity through time and space."[40]

The Leakeys found their Oldowan tools alongside *Australopithecus* fossils, but they did not believe that the *Australopithecus* was intelligent enough to make them. Howell says that this was a common belief at the time:

> One itchy problem that tickled persistently in the minds of the paleoanthropologists was the problem of tools and who used them. The more familiar the investigators became with [different types of] robust australopithecines, the more certain it appeared that they were more primitive than the [gracile australopithecines] whose brain was relatively larger and whose jaws and teeth were smaller and more delicate. So long as the only association between australopithecine fossils and tools had been the inconclusive evidence from

South Africa, it seemed safe to assume that [the gracile australopithecus] was the user. But Leakey's discovery of an extremely ancient robust type in a site full of tools turned that assumption upside-down. Now, on the basis of the clear stratigraphic association at Olduvai, the more primitive-appearing of the two species also seemed to be the tool user. But that didn't make sense, and the itch wouldn't go away.[41]

Howell believes that this problem was solved when the Leakeys found fossils from a previously undiscovered species in 1960. They named this species *Homo habilis*, or "handy man," because they believed it was the first user of tools. Many scientists agree that *Homo habilis* made and used Oldowan tools; however, this issue is still not resolved. Richard Klein says:

> One vexing question that remains unsatisfactorily answered is, who made Oldowan tools? The possible candidates are robust australopithecines and early *Homo* (or the immediate ancestor of early *Homo*), both of which are broadly contemporaneous with the Oldowan. In [one location] at Olduvai Gorge, remains of a robust australopithecine and of *H. habilis* have even been found with Oldowan tools on the same ancient [site]. . . . No one doubts that *H. habilis* was responsible for many of the tools, since it (or one of the constituents into which it may ultimately be split) was ancestral to later tool-making hominids. The issue is whether the robust australopithecines also produced some of the tools.[42]

Klein offers some evidence that the robust australopithecines were capable of making tools.

A montage of articles, research papers, and fossils document the Leakeys' 1960 discovery of Homo habilis. Habilis *may have been the first hominid to use tools.*

In favor of robust-australopithecine tool manufacture, there is the repeated, although rudimentary, use and manufacture of tools by chimpanzees, suggesting that a similar proclivity characterized the common ancestor of chimpanzees and hominids and thus all early hominids. Moreover, unlike chimpanzees and earlier australopithecines, at least *Australopithecus robustus* apparently had hands that were well adapted for precision grasping, facilitating tool use and manufacture. In fact . . . its hands did not differ significantly from those of *H. habilis* and later members of the genus *Homo*. . . . However, if both early *Homo* and the robust australopithecines made tools, we might expect to find two distinct, contemporaneous tool-making traditions.[43]

However, Klein explains that whoever used Oldowan tools eventually developed more sophisticated ways to make them, and none of these advanced tools appeared at a time when australopithecines existed. He therefore finds it likely that *Homo habilis* and its ancestors were the sole users of these tools, saying:

The implication is that the robust australopithecines made relatively few, if any, chipped stone artifacts. Their limited reliance on stone tools (if it

Brain Size

Some scientists have made assumptions about the intelligence of a hominid species based on the size of its brain. However, as Donald Johanson and Maitland Edey point out in their book Lucy, *brain size is not a reliable measure of intelligence.*

"It is clear that preoccupation with brain size can be misleading. It becomes even clearer when we learn that differences in brain size within our [modern human] species appear to have no significant correlation with the intelligence of their owners. Rather, they reflect differences in body size. Big men have big brains, but they are no smarter than small men. Men are also larger than women and have consistently larger brains, but the two sexes are of equal intelligence."

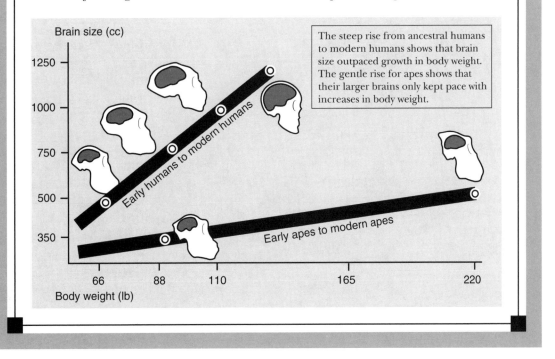

The steep rise from ancestral humans to modern humans shows that brain size outpaced growth in body weight. The gentle rise for apes shows that their larger brains only kept pace with increases in body weight.

existed) may have been correlated with their emphasis on vegetal food and on powerful jaws to process it, as well as with their failure to develop larger brains. Conversely, an increasing dependence on stone tools may be strongly related to the reduced jaws, enlarged brain, and probable greater carnivory of early *Homo*. Very likely, an enlarged brain, reduced jaws, and increased carnivory also promoted greater stone-tool use, which may thus have been both cause and effect in the emergence and ongoing evolution of *Homo*.[44]

Homo Habilis **Behavior**

In the years since the Leakeys' discovery of the first *Homo habilis* fossils, many more have been uncovered, both in eastern Africa and in South Africa. These fossils give scientists a good idea of what this species looked like. Except for its brain size and jaw structure, it appeared similar to *Australopithecus*. Both creatures walked upright and were approximately the same height and weight.

Because of these similarities, some scientists believe that the *Homo habilis* evolved from a type of *Australopithecus*. Others believe that each species evolved separately. In fact, Klein says that "specialists cannot agree on which species and how many species existed at any one time."[45] Nonetheless, he reports that the prevailing view is that *Homo habilis* appeared approximately 2 million years ago and disappeared approximately 1.8–1.7 million years ago, while *Australopithecus* appeared approximately 4 million years ago and disappeared between 1 million and 700,000 years ago. No one knows what caused *Homo habilis* to disappear, but many scientists, including Klein, believe that this species evolved into a subsequent form of hominid, *Homo erectus*.

A reconstruction of a sickle shows how early hominids may have used stone and bone to fashion tools. This modern re-creation uses three flint blades inserted into an animal bone.

From a study of fossil artifacts, scientists have made assumptions about the way *habilis* lived. For example, Klein says that experiments on nine Oldowan tools show that "three . . . were used for scraping or sawing wood, four for cutting meat, and two for cutting grass stems or reeds."[46] In addition, the concentration of these tools in one location indicates that *Homo habilis* lived together in a primitive village, which implies certain other behaviors. Klein reports some archaeologists' beliefs:

> The repeated use of a "home base" or "base camp" where garbage accumulates is a uniquely human (vs. ape) behavioral trait and . . . implies other distinctively human traits, such as food sharing among group members and a division of labor between the sexes. Accepting Oldowan artifact/bone concentrations as home bases therefore indicates that an important constellation of typically human behavior patterns appeared at least 2 [million years ago].[47]

However, many scientists disagree with this description of *Homo habilis* life. In fact, most aspects of *Homo habilis* behavior remain in dispute. Some scientists think that these creatures hunted large animals, while others think they were only capable of hunting small ones. Some believe they could talk, while others think this is unlikely. In comparison to other *Homo* species, the *habilis* did not survive long enough to offer paleoanthropologists enough evidence about its lifestyle. Much more is known about *Homo erectus*, the creature into which *Homo habilis* evolved.

3 The Lower Paleolithic Period: *Homo Erectus*

Homo erectus, the "upright man," first appeared approximately 1.8 million years ago, and it was the dominant hominid species through the remainder of the Lower Paleolithic Period. Moreover, unlike the *Australopithecus* and the *Homo habilis*, *Homo erectus* has been found not only throughout the entire African continent but in other world regions as well.

Java Man

In fact, the first *Homo erectus* fossils were discovered on the island of Java, which was part of Indonesia. They were found in 1887 by a Dutch anatomist named Eugene Dubois, who had convinced the Dutch East Indian government of the island to allow him to excavate an area where many types of monkeys lived.

Dubois had abandoned a teaching career to search for fossil evidence that humans and apes had evolved from a common ancestor. For both practical and scientific reasons, Dubois believed that Java was a good place to start his search. John Reader describes the early part of Dubois's work:

> Dubois's proposal to the government had called for a systematic, widespread survey, and he did indeed travel exten-

sively on his preliminary explorations, but before long his attention was almost exclusively devoted to the Kendeng deposits at the foot of Mount Lawu, an occasionally active volcano standing about thirty-two kilometres west of Mount Willis. In trial excavations throughout the Kendeng deposits his workmen found many vertebrate fossils, some in quite large accumulations. This led Dubois to believe that the animals had been killed simultaneously by volcanic action and that their bodies and bones had been swept together by flood waters down ancient rivers, to be deposited in calm pools and on sharp bends. The quantity and variety of the fossil fauna Dubois's expedition recovered from the Kendeng is most impressive. It includes fish and reptiles, elephants, rhinoceros, hippopotamus and tapir, deer, cats and a giant pangolin. In all, more than 12,000 fossils were collected, filling more than 400 cases when they were shipped back to Holland and holding a wealth of information on the fauna and environment of prehistoric Java.[48]

Eventually Dubois also found two unusual fossils: a tooth and a skull cap that appeared to be from a strange kind of

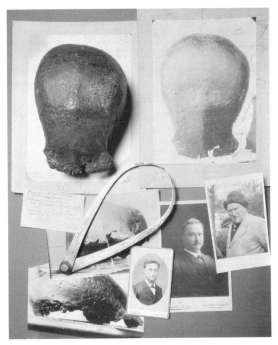

A composite photograph combines pictures of Eugene Dubois with photos of the skull cap of his fossil find, Pithecanthropus erectus, *popularly known as Java Man.* Pithecanthropus *was later renamed* Homo erectus.

The points of contention were quite straightforward. If the remains had belonged to one individual, as Dubois claimed, then they represented an ape, a man, or the intermediate ape-man that Dubois proposed. But not everyone agreed that the fossils had belonged to one individual, which considerably increased the number of interpretations; and the question could never be proved one way or another. It was more a matter of probability than of fact, and in considering it, the protagonists were free to choose the facts they thought more probable. Dubois, for example, ignored his own assertion that the Kendeng fossil accumulations were the jumbled remains of many volcano victims, while his critics ignored

A front and side view reveal the reconstructed skull of Java Man. Eugene Dubois believed that this hominid was the missing developmental link between apes and humans.

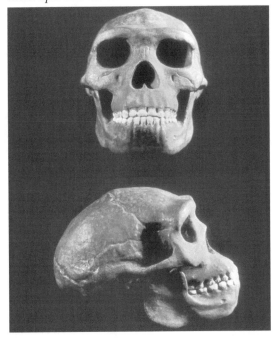

chimpanzee. Then he found a fossilized thighbone in the same general area; the thigh was definitely from some type of early human. Later he found a jawbone that seemed primatelike. Dubois decided that all of these fossils were from the same creature, and he believed he had found the Missing Link. At first he named it *Anthropopithecus erectus,* or "upright manlike ape," but he later changed it to *Pithecanthropus erectus,* "upright apelike man." It wasn't until the 1940s, when most scientists accepted the species as a member of the *Homo* genus, that its name was changed to *Homo erectus.*

Dubois's discovery was nicknamed the "Java Man," and it immediately caused a great deal of controversy. Reader says:

the observation that the four fossils were the only primate remains among thousands of fossils recovered from the [area], which Dubois felt was enough to prove their association.[49]

Peking Man

Dubois firmly believed that Java Man was the Missing Link. But soon scientists discovered convincing evidence that *Homo erectus* was an early form of human rather than any kind of ape.

This evidence came from an important archaeological site in China. It was an abandoned lime mine called Chou K'ou Tien, now named Zhoukoudian, which was near the city of Peking (now Beijing) in northern China. Scientists excavating the Zhoukoudian cave between the years 1927 and 1937 found fossilized bones, particularly skull pieces and teeth, from approximately forty-five *Homo erectus*. They named their discovery "Peking Man."

Once scientists had assembled an entire skull of *Homo erectus*, they were able to draw conclusions about its relationship to

apes. Archaeologist Richard Leakey, son of Louis and Mary Leakey, describes the appearance of a complete *Homo erectus* skull in his book with Roger Lewin, *Origins Reconsidered*, saying:

The salient [outstanding] characteristic of this species, which allows us to recognize it from small fossil fragments, is the long, low cranium, housing a brain two-thirds the size of modern brains, and sporting prominent ridges of bone above the eye sockets, the so-called brow ridges. The forehead is flat, and the back of the cranium is curiously bun-shaped. Although the face juts out more than it does in modern humans, it does so less than in earlier hominids and in apes. When I hold a *Homo erectus* cranium in my hand and look at it full face, I get a strong feeling of being in the presence of something distinctly human. It is the first point in human history at which a real humanness impresses itself so forcefully.

It is true, I know, that the probable immediate ancestor of *Homo erectus*, a species called *Homo habilis*, is in many

A photograph compares the skull of a gorilla (left) to the skulls of Peking Man (center) and a modern human (right). Most scientists agree that both Java Man and Peking Man belonged to the species Homo erectus.

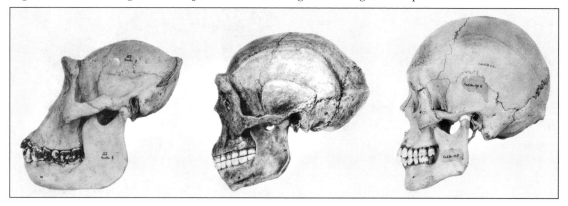

Tools as Trash

Scientists have spent a great deal of time identifying and classifying Stone Age tools. However, in his book The Neandertal Enigma, *James Shreeve suggests that these tools might not offer a true representation of what early hominids actually used to perform their daily tasks.*

"If ancient populations behaved like modern ones, most of the artifacts in an archaeological assemblage are not the fresh, keen-edged tools that bit into flesh or whittled a wooden spear, but the discarded end products of a history of use. A tool might be used initially to chop up a tuber [edible root], then resharpened along another edge to scrape a hide, and finally, after that edge went dull, retouched again to form a point that could be used to dig marrow out of a bone. All through its life cycle, the same piece of stone assumes different forms, any one of which might be the last—and hence the one that an archaeologist would pick up a hundred millennia later, confident that what he had found had some intrinsic formal meaning. Ironically, it might be the only part of the original stone that *couldn't* be used as a tool."

ways simply a smaller-brained version. And it is true that when I look at a skull of this species, I cannot mistake it for that of an ape or one of the small-brained early hominids. But in a sense difficult to explain, *Homo erectus* seems to have "arrived," to be at the threshold of something extremely important in our history.[50]

The scientists who discovered Peking Man believed that it was a member of the same species as Java Man. They therefore disputed Dubois's Missing Link theory. According to John Reader,

The similarities [between the newly discovered Peking Man and Dubois's Java Man] far exceeded the differences that Dubois would have stressed. The

new specimens matched what there was of Dubois's fossils and supplied enough of what was missing to satisfy everyone else that the Java and Peking fossils all represented an early form of man, with almost nothing of the ape about him. *Pithecanthropus erectus* was not an ape-man.[51]

Dubois never accepted this view. Until his death in 1940, he continued to insist that Java Man and Peking Man represented two different species. However, most scientists now agree that both must have been *Homo erectus.*

Part of their opinion was based on secondhand evidence. In 1941 American scientists made detailed notes, photographs, drawings, and casts of the Peking Man fossils, but during World War II the bones themselves mysteriously disappeared, and no one knows what happened to them. Fortunately, though, several more *Homo erectus* fossils were found in the Zhoukoudian cave after the war. In addition, other *Homo erectus* fossils have subsequently been found elsewhere in Asia, as well as in Europe and Africa.

The Northern Migration

Homo erectus fossils found at different locations have different ages. Scientists estimate that Peking Man lived between 400,000 and 600,000 years ago, a time when they believed that the island of Java was connected to the mainland of southeast Asia. Java Man might have existed for a longer time span. Fossils found in recent years suggest that this *Homo erectus* might have been on earth from 1.8 million years ago to 700,000 years ago; *Homo erectus* fossils from Spain seem to be 700,000 years old, and scientists have found one *Homo erectus* jawbone in Russia, near the Black and Caspian Seas, that might be as old as 1.8 million years.

The largest number of very old *Homo erectus* fossils come from Africa. One of the oldest of these is a nearly complete male skeleton from northern Kenya. Found at a site called Nariokotome on Lake Turkana, it is called the "Turkana boy" and is estimated to be 1.6 million years old. Scientist Holly Smith of the University of Michigan has studied the Turkana boy and believes that he was approximately eleven years old at the time of his death.

The first *Homo erectus* fossils were found in Africa in 1949, in an area called Swartkrans, and in 1965 Louis and Mary

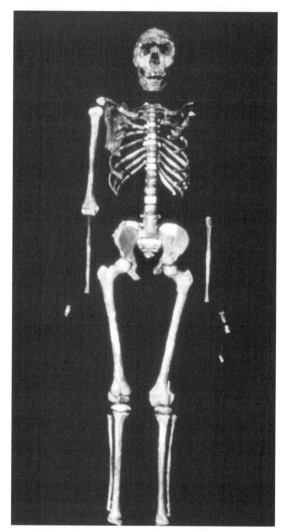

The skeleton of Turkana boy is estimated to be 1.6 million years old.

Leakey came upon the species at the Olduvai Gorge. Through these and other discoveries, most of which are older than the more plentiful Asian and European *Homo erectus* fossils, many scientists believe that the species began in Africa and eventually migrated elsewhere, over land bridges that no longer exist. This northern migration consequently exposed the hominids to new climate conditions. As Richard Klein says:

Like *H. habilis* and the australopithecines, early *H. erectus* was apparently confined to Africa, but about 1 [million years ago] or shortly before, it dispersed to Eurasia, and the majority of known *H. erectus* fossils come from the Far East. In Africa, *H. erectus* eventually colonized some relatively dry regions that had previously been unoccupied, and in parts of Eurasia, it became the first hominid species to adapt to truly cool-temperate conditions.[52]

The reasons for this migration are unclear. However, biological anthropologist Robert Foley believes that scientists can make certain assumptions about them.

I'm not sure that any *Homo erectus* population or family or even a single brave individual ever set off to colonize the world. In fact, I'm 90 percent certain that never happened. But when we look at successful populations, be they human or animal, what happens is that population growth puts pressure on resources—and then populations are faced with the choice of either [coping with life in a more crowded area] or else finding somewhere else to live.[53]

But whatever the reasons for these migrations, Klein suggests that they might have helped *Homo erectus* evolve into a more intelligent species than its ancestors,

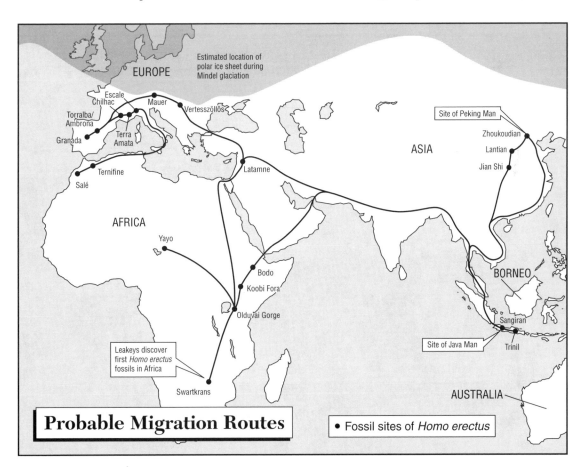

Probable Migration Routes

• Fossil sites of *Homo erectus*

because it had to learn to adapt to ever-changing environmental conditions. Perhaps this is why the *Homo erectus* was the first hominid to understand the importance of fire.

Acquiring and Cooking Meat

While some scientists believe that *Homo habilis* might have taken advantage of the heat and light of naturally occurring fires in limited ways, most have concluded that it was *Homo erectus* who first used fire for cooking and heating. The best evidence for this was found in the Zhoukoudian cave, where prehistoric ash beds and charcoal exist alongside the human fossils. Klein says that while some of these ashes might have been from a natural fire, others definitely "represent true fossil hearths."[54] The existence of hearths also suggests certain shared communal activities, which scientist Roger Lewin calls "home bases, places to which food was brought, shared, and consumed . . . a very un-ape-like behavior."[55]

These hearths contain burnt animal bones, which indicates that *Homo erectus* ate cooked meat. However, scientists disagree on what kinds of animals these were and on whether or not *Homo erectus* was a scavenger, much like *Homo habilis*. The animal bones found in the Zhoukoudian cave do reflect a wide variety of species, including several species of deer, which suggests that *Homo erectus* did eat large as well as small game. But it is also possible that the larger animal bones were brought to the cave by later occupants: hyenas, whose remains have also been found there.

A painting depicts Homo erectus *using fire to cook a meal. Scientists believe that this hominid species was the first to actively use fire for cooking and heating.*

Klein says that scientists are still trying to determine how hyenas affected the archaeological site:

> There are layers at Zhoukoudian, particularly near the top of the deposit, where evidence for hyenas is rare or absent and evidence for people (artifacts, hearths, etc.) is especially abundant. . . . Fresh excavations now underway may provide [information] from which it will eventually be possible to infer whether *Homo erectus* was truly an accomplished hunter.[56]

Types of Tools

At the time the Zhoukoudian cave was discovered, many scientists believed that the existence of prehistoric tools at *Homo erectus* fossil sites proved that this species was a hunter, particularly because many of these tools seem to have been used for butchering animals. But now most scientists agree that tools alone cannot indicate truths about behavior. For example, in discussing hominid tools, archaeologist Lewis Binford says: "In a technical sense we as archaeologists don't have any facts. In science a fact is defined as the property or characteristic of an event. And the events that we are interested in, we can't observe."[57] He points out that butchering and hunting are two separate behaviors that are not necessarily related.

> When they found the stone tools with the bones, the inference was made quickly that they were . . . hunting. . . . But the work I had done with ethnographic peoples in Africa, particularly in the Kalahari region, where they reg-

ularly scavenge off lion kills, suggested that there was another possibility. That they weren't killing many of these animals, but were . . . scavenging and stealing.[58]

Moreover, scientists cannot agree on the functions of various Stone Age tools. As Richard Klein explains,

> Their functions are speculative, based on resemblances to historic tools of known function or on feasibility experiments with modern replicas. . . . Limited understanding of the way(s) in which many ancient stone artifacts were used remains a major obstacle to a fuller understanding of ancient human behavior.[59]

Nonetheless, scientists have made certain assumptions about how these tools were made and used, and they have classified them accordingly. First, they have identified two basic types: core tools and flake tools. Core tools were made from a core form, which is simply a pebble or rock fragment from which smaller pieces of rock, called flakes, have been chipped. The chipping or flaking process, called *knapping*, created either one or two sharp edges on the core form. Core tools with one sharp edge are called *unifacial*; those with two sharp edges are called *bifacial.* Scientists have designated unifacial core tools as choppers, whereas bifacial ones are either hand axes or cleavers. However, some core forms were not used as tools at all. They were only a source of flakes, and were discarded after knapping.

Flakes had many different shapes, depending upon the type of knapping process used to create them. In some cases, the core form was struck with a hammer stone to remove a flake. In other cases, the core form was placed on a stationary hammer stone, or anvil, and struck with an antler or other object. Sometimes instead of striking the core with an antler, the toolmaker used pressure to scrape off a flake; however, this was a more sophisticated process and was not used by *Homo erectus* but by its descendants.

Regardless of how they were created, flake tools were easy to hold and had a variety of purposes. Scientists have identified several different kinds of flake tools, including borers, blades, and scrapers, that might have been used to prepare animal hides for wearing.

Industrial Complexes and Culture

Scientists who study Stone Age tools group these artifacts according to the toolmakers' manufacturing techniques, using a classification system established by a nineteenth-century archaeologist named Gabriel de Mortillet. Mortillet believed that a culture could be identified by its tool technology. Therefore the name of each tool technology, or "industrial complex," also represents a specific time period and culture.

The oldest industrial complex, or culture, is the Acheulean, which was first identified at St. Acheul beside the Somme River in northern France. Acheulean flake tools include scrapers, sidescrapers, borers, and backed knives, and Acheulean core tools include many different types of hand axes. The oldest Acheulean tools, used approximately 1.5 million years ago, have been discovered in Africa, primarily at the Olduvai Gorge site. Their technology appears to have developed from the primitive Oldowan tools used by *Homo habilis*. However, Acheulean tools are typically found alongside *Homo erectus* fossils; therefore scientists believe that only *Homo erectus* used them.

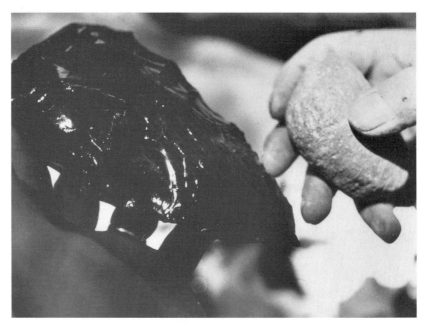

An archaeologist demonstrates how Homo habilis *and* Homo erectus *used stones to create flake tools. Scientists surmise that early hominids used flake tools to perform many tasks, including preparing hides for use as clothing.*

This stone chopper from the Acheulean culture, which was found at Olduvai Gorge, is estimated to be 700,000 years old.

Some of the most primitive Acheulean tools found in Europe were originally clas-ified as separate industrial complexes, the Abbevillian and the Chellean, but now scientists consider these part of the Acheulean culture. The Abbevillian tools, which include both crude flakes and thick hand axes, were first discovered along the Somme River in 1836, near the town of Abbeville, France. The Chellean tools, which are strictly hand axes, were also found along the river, near Chelles, France. Together these two industries were used from over 1 million to approximately 500,000 years ago.

Overall, the Acheulean culture lasted from 1.5 million years ago to 200,000 years ago. It began in Africa and spread through Europe and Asia as *Homo erectus* migrated north. But approximately 700,000 years ago, the industry evolved to include a technique called the Levalloisian (or Levallois), which was a more complicated form of flaking. To create a Levalloisian flake, the knapper had to prepare the core form carefully, planning each strike of the hammer stone.

This more sophisticated technique formed the bridge to a new industrial complex, the Mousterian. The Mousterian culture appeared at the beginning of the Middle Paleolithic Period, along with a new hominid: *Homo sapiens*, which means "wise humans."

4 The Middle Paleolithic Period: Archaic *Homo Sapiens* and Neandertal Man

The first *Homo sapiens*, called "archaic *Homo sapiens*," first appeared in Africa, Europe, and east Asia about 500,000 years ago. Not much is currently known about this species, but scientists continue to collect and study its fossils.

One of the oldest *Homo sapiens* fossils is a partial skull and collection of bones found in 1921 at a site called Broken Hill (now Kabwe), near Zambia in southern Africa. These bones, which are estimated to be about 200,000 to 400,000 years old, indicate that the person's death was caused by an ear infection. Today, with antibiotics readily available, few people in developed countries die of ear infections. Left untreated, however, such a disease can destroy bone tissue and progress into the brain.

Another archaic *Homo sapiens* skull was discovered in 1933 at Steinheim, Germany. The Steinheim fossil is from an adult female who lived approximately 200,000 to 300,000 years ago. Archaeologists also found a male skull estimated to be from the same time period at the Petralona Cave in Greece.

Some people think that this species might be even older. In 1994 scientists working in Ceprano, Italy, found bone fragments from a skull that they estimate to be 800,000 to 900,000 years old. They

have tentatively identified this skull as *Homo erectus* because it exhibits several *erectus* features. However, it also has a larger braincase than classic *erectus* skulls, so some scientists believe it might be some form of archaic *Homo sapiens* instead.

Archaeologist Richard Klein explains that archaic *Homo sapiens* was "distinguished from *Homo erectus* mainly by a larger braincase" and that otherwise "in all detectable aspects of behavior, early *Homo sapiens* seems to have been generally similar to *H. erectus*."[60] Klein believes that archaic *Homo sapiens* did not migrate into regions unknown to *Homo erectus*, nor did it obtain food or use tools in new ways.

However, recent discoveries suggest that archaic *Homo sapiens* did use tools differently. For example, whereas scientists believe that *Homo erectus*, if it hunted at all, killed animals at close range, new evidence suggests that archaic *Homo sapiens* hunted large game from a distance. In 1995 scientists discovered 400,000-year-old spears at a site near Schoningen, Germany, and according to site archaeologist Hartmut Thieme, these spears were clearly used for throwing: "The heavier weight at the front of the spear tells us it was made to be thrown from a distance rather than thrust at close range."[61]

Homo Heidelbergensis and Homo Neanderthalensis

Archaeologists have also discovered 500,000-year-old horse fossils that indicate these animals might have been hunted by early humans. Archaeologist Mark Roberts, who was involved with one of these discoveries in England, explains:

> Horses may have moved up and down the coast in herds. Almost certainly humans would have been hunting them cooperatively, rather than scavenging them. We believe that because we never find butchery marks on top of the tooth marks of scavenging animals. It's always the other way around.[62]

In other words, the horses were killed and butchered *before* scavenging animals moved in to chew on their bones.

The early human species associated with these horse fossils is called the *Homo heidel-bergensis*, but this name is in dispute. Some scientists believe that *Homo heidelbergensis* is actually a type of *Homo erectus*, while others believe it is an archaic *Homo sapiens*. In any case, the name is derived from a fossilized mandible bone discovered in 1907 at a place called Mauer, near Heidelberg, Germany. Approximately 400,000 to 700,000 years old, the Mauer mandible, or jawbone, resembles mandibles from *Homo erectus*, yet its molar teeth resemble those of archaic *Homo sapiens*. Similar fossils in the same age range have since been found in Italy, Spain, Great Britain, and Ethiopia.

But the best known early *Homo sapiens* is the *Homo sapiens neanderthalensis*. Like the *Homo heidelbergensis*, this species is sometimes thought to be separate from the family of *Homo sapiens*. Therefore some scientists call it simply *Homo neanderthalensis*, or, more commonly, Neandertal Man.

Quarrymen found the first Neandertal fossils in 1856 while excavating a cave in the Neander Valley near Düsseldorf,

An illustration attempts to re-create the appearance of the Homo sapiens *who lived at the site known as Broken Hill in southern Africa.*

Germany. Since then, many more Neandertal fossils have been discovered in Europe, Russia, the Middle East, western Asia, and Great Britain. None have yet been found in Africa, and most scientists believe that Neandertals never lived there.

Neandertals first appeared in Europe approximately 130,000 years ago and spread into western Asia approximately 75,000 years ago. Thus, they lived during a time when the earth's climate was particularly harsh. According to Richard Leakey,

Neandertals first appear in the fossil record when the world was relatively warm. This was . . . when there was a warm period between two cold spells of the Ice Ages. But the last Ice Age be-

Archaic *Homo Sapiens* in Europe

A museum exhibit depicts a Neandertal family. Neandertals were remarkably resilient, living on Earth for approximately sixty thousand years.

gan about 70,000 years ago, so during most of their existence the Neandertals were experiencing one of the coldest spells the world has ever known.[63]

New Behaviors

However, from the large number of fossils and artifacts the Neandertals left behind, scientists know that this species found a way to survive on earth for approximately 60,000 years. Evidence indicates that they used fire, ate a great deal of cooked meat, and made animal skins into clothing, all of which helped them to keep warm. As members of the Mousterian culture, they made over sixty different kinds of tools, and they built their own shelters when caves were not available.

Moreover, Neandertals were the first hominids to bury their dead. This in itself would be significant, but there is an additional element to Neandertal burials: The way they were performed indicates that they might have had a ceremonial aspect. Richard Leakey explains:

There are signs in the way they buried their dead that the Neandertals recognized a spiritual aspect to life. At Le

Moustier in France, a teenage boy was buried lying on his side with his head resting on his arms. A pile of flints lay under his head and a beautiful stone axe lay near his hand. All around him were the bones of wild cattle. It is easy to imagine that these things were put in his grave to help him on his way after death.[64]

Leakey describes other Neandertal burials, including one where "dense clusters of fossil pollen show that flowers were arranged around the body making a colorful grave of white, yellow and blue. The flowers are all medicinal herbs, suggesting the possibility that the man was some sort of doctor and these were the herbs he used in his medicines."[65]

Such behavior suggests that Neandertals might have been more intelligent than their predecessors. In addition, they had a large braincase; in fact, their brains were larger than modern humans. But the Neandertal body was also far shorter and more muscular, and some scientists suggest that the Neandertal required a larger brain simply to control this heavy musculature.

Anthropologist Richard Klein supports this view, believing that despite its new behaviors, Neandertal Man was in fact no

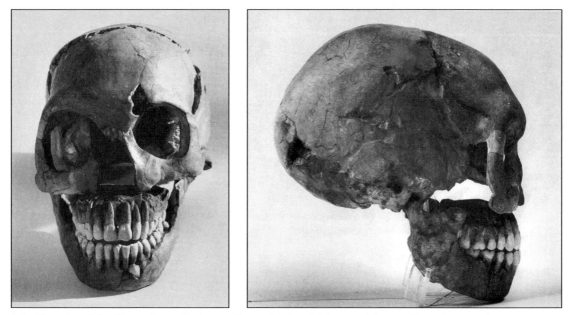

The Neandertal skull has a larger braincase than other hominids, as evident in these photographs. Neandertals' larger brain size may have been necessary to control their extremely muscular bodies.

more intelligent than *Homo erectus*. In arguing his belief that early *Homo sapiens* "remained similar to their predecessors and very unlike their anatomically modern successors,"[66] he points out that the Middle Paleolithic Period was noted for its lack of innovation. Once Neandertals developed the Mousterian toolmaking tradition, they never changed it.

Mobility

However, James Shreeve believes there might be another reason that Neandertals continued to make tools in the same way: a lack of mobility. He explains that during the Upper Paleolithic Period, when tool styles were continually changing, people traveled widely and interacted with a large number of strangers. They therefore de-

rived a sense of pride from their toolmaking skills, and also used them as a form of group identity. In other words, someone who made tools in a particular way would be immediately recognized as coming from a particular tribe and a particular location. Shreeve offers this example:

Imagine two [Upper] Paleolithic hunting parties meeting in some border area between their separate territories. Their two clans are knit together by a history of reciprocal exchanges and common traditions, including a particular way of fashioning spearpoints. This common point of reference allows them to meet without hostility: *"Ah, I see by your spear that you are of the River People. Seen any deer?"* Suppose one of the groups later encounters a third hunting party, whose weapons look different. Even if the others never intended their spearpoints to "say" anything when they made them, the weapons will transmit a distinct social message to the River People: *"Weird spear! Not River People!"* and probably *"Watch out!"* [67]

In contrast, based on a study of *neanderthalensis* body structure and fossil evidence, many scientists believe that Neandertals did not travel outside of a limited territory. Therefore the appearance of their tools would not matter as long as they functioned well. As archaeologist John Shea says,

> [For Neandertals] there wouldn't be any question that you belong to the resident hominid group, because you are *there*, the only one in this valley, this cave, this range, this part of the coast, or whatever. It's only when you have lots of contact, lots of people around, that these messages of identity become important. [68]

Therefore a lack of creative toolmaking does not necessarily mean that Neandertals were of limited intelligence.

Moreover, some scientists believe that Neandertal tools themselves do reflect intelligence. For example, Shea believes that Mousterian spear tips would not have worked properly had they merely been tied to an ordinary stick. Instead the spear shafts had to be shaped to hold the tips. Shreeve reports:

> Shea discovered . . . that cutting a beveled shelf out in the tip of a spear-shaft and laying the opposite, concave side of the point against it created a very cozy fit. So perhaps the Neandertals were modifying the shafts to fit the unwieldy shape of their Levallois points. "Slop in some pine pitch, lash it

tight with leather or sinew, and you have a very effective projectile. Especially if you happen to be a Neandertal with the upper body strength to make an Olympic javelin champion look puny." [69]

Planning Depth

However, preparing a shaft requires careful planning, and some scientists do not believe that Neandertals were capable of such thinking. For example, archaeologist Lewis Binford says that Neandertals were completely unlike modern humans precisely because they could not plan. According to James Shreeve,

> What [Binford] thinks Neandertals and other archaic *sapiens* lacked most acutely is a distinctly human quality he has named "planning depth." Modern humans constantly perform actions whose benefit will be realized only in the future. Fishing societies, for instance, will move themselves to a camp by a seasonal salmon run well before the salmon get there themselves. . . . On the other hand, Middle Paleolithic hominids . . . seem to have subsisted in the now. [70]

Binford supports this view with fossil evidence that Neandertals failed to eat salmon, even though it seasonally appeared beside many of their cave dwellings. They also failed to take advantage of seasonal deer migrations. Shreeve says that if these people were hunters, "they did not seem to be responding much to movements of the hunted. Instead, they were taking whatever happened to wander inside their territory." [71]

Moreover, Binford does not believe that Neandertals hunted large game, because this would have required planning.

However, other scientists disagree, particularly considering Mark Roberts's and others' discoveries of early *Homo sapiens* throwing spears. Shreeve says:

> Most archaeologists grant Neandertals and other Middle Paleolithic people more hunting prowess, and considerably deeper planning abilities. If . . . Neandertals were throwing spears, it is hard to imagine what they were throwing them at, if not game. In some places . . . many archaeologists see the piled-up bones of bovids, horses, and

Neandertal men use primitive spears to hunt a bear. Scientists believe that Neandertals hunted in groups to increase their chances of killing large game.

reindeer beneath a steep cliff as the aftermath of a "cliff drive," a cooperative and therefore planned hunting technique often used by Paleo-Indians of the New World.[72]

Cliff-drive sites indicate that humans had to work together to force an animal herd to its death. Similarly, archaeologist Alison Brooks has found a site where a large number of hunters killed larger game such as zebra and giant buffalo, which would have required teamwork. Shreeve wonders whether this site might be "some sort of aggregation spot where human groups came at a fixed time of year to hunt game and exchange information. If so, they were acting not like Middle Stone Age hominids are supposed to but like modern hunter-gatherers."[73]

Other evidence of Neandertal hunting practices also indicates some level of intelligent creativity. In particular, Shreeve points to the studies of archaeologist Mary Stiner, who analyzed animal bones from four Middle Paleolithic sites:

> [Stiner] discovered that Neandertals in the early part of that time period, roughly from 110,000 to 65,000 years ago, were hunting much like other large carnivores: ambushing whatever prey they happened to come across and killing only the easily captured weak and young. Much of their meat may have been scavenged. But as the climate turned colder with the glacial advance, *these* Neandertals abruptly shifted their predatory pattern and began killing prime adult prey instead. Stiner speculates that this fundamental shift was occasioned by a greater metabolic need for fat, triggered by the increasing cold. But no matter what the cause, they were

An illustration depicts how the interior of a Neandertal cave may have appeared. Neandertals are believed to have lived communally in groups of approximately twenty-five individuals. Many scientists conclude, however, that these more permanent communities comprised mainly women and children.

capturing a more dangerous, difficult prey with the same old Middle Paleolithic tool kit, implying a greater reliance on something else to make the kill—probably increased social interaction and cooperation. In this case it was not the technology but the hunting strategy that was modernized.[74]

Caring for the Family

Some scientists believe the Neandertals applied this increased social interaction not only to their hunting behavior but to family life as well. From fossil evidence they have concluded that Neandertals lived in groups of about twenty-five individuals and that Neandertal males and childless females hunted and brought back meat to mothers, children, and those not well enough to hunt, all of whom remained behind in a common dwelling. In support of this position, science writer George Constable offers this depiction of Neandertal life:

> The sun is hanging just above the horizon when a triumphant parade of Neandertal men and women reaches home again, carrying armloads of meat. . . . Later, after the meal is over and darkness has descended, the entire band huddles around the fire. A baby sleeps in his mother's arms; a man begins to nod.[75]

However, other scientists believe that Neandertal males lived a nomadic life, and only returned "home" when they wanted to mate. The rest of the time, the Neandertal women were left behind to forage and care for the tribe's children on their own. This theory is based in part on research at a Neandertal site called Combe Grenal in the Dordogne region of France. According to James Shreeve,

Some experts assert that Neandertal men were primarily nomadic hunters who lived separate from Neandertal women and did not provide for their families.

The horizontal layers of Combe Grenal bespeak a quite different social organization, over and over again with a numbing redundancy through . . . 75,000 years [of occupation by Neandertals]. In each level, there seem to be two separate sorts of activity areas. . . . It would appear that the cave is being shared by one group of people who are highly mobile, moving over substantial territory, and another group of people who are "sitting" on the resources available in the immediate area, eating plant foods and scavenged animal bits.[76]

Shreeve reports that Lewis Binford and several other archaeologists have therefore concluded that "Neandertal women and children . . . were pretty much making it on their own."[77] Shreeve concludes:

The dividing difference between Neandertal males and their modern counterparts is that moderns bring what they catch back to be shared with the women and children. The Neandertals—at least the ones who chose to occupy Combe Grenal for seventy-five millennia—were not so generous. They might well have been *catching* game, or scavenging successfully—but they weren't transporting it back to share with the females and the young. Most of the time, the males were dining—and living—somewhere else. The odd head parts and marrow bones that they *did* bring into the cave may simply have been tidbits requiring more processing to squeeze out their food value: limb joints that could be heated to release their succulent grease, bones to be dried out before marrow could be extracted, skulls to be broken open so the rich brain-food could be fingered out. Perhaps some of these scraps were shared with the nest-dwellers, but not to the extent that they could depend on them.[78]

This opinion seems to be supported by Neandertal musculature. Female Neandertals were as strong as male ones, which implies that they worked hard to attain their own food and defend their young. However, many scientists, including Czechoslovakian archaeologist Jiri Svoboda, disagree with the idea that so much could be inferred from the separate dwelling areas within the Combe Grenal. Shreeve quotes Svoboda as stating: "What you are saying, this is impossible to believe."[79]

Human Speech

One of the arguments for a more complex Neandertal society, where men and women interacted on a regular basis, involves the development of speech. Some scientists believe that *Homo sapiens* was different from its predecessors in that it was able to talk and thereby communicate complex ideas.

For example, Mark Roberts believes that for *Homo heidelbergensis* to have hunted horses, it must have been able to work together and communicate in spoken language in order to plan complicated tactics in advance. He says, "Before [discovering the horse fossils], we doubted that humans had speech this early. But for this kind of group hunting, which would require strategies such as ambush, speech would have been critical."[80]

For years, the prevailing view among scientists was that early *Homo sapiens* had its larynx, or voice box, positioned too high in the throat, so it could not talk. Some scientists continue to believe this, but recent fossil evidence might suggest otherwise. Science writer James Shreeve reports that in 1983 archaeologists working on a 60,000-year-old site in Israel discovered a fossilized skeleton that included both the jaw and a throat bone called the *hyoid*, which together indicate that early *Homo sapiens* could speak.

According to anatomist Jeffrey Laitman,

If you have the jaw, and you know the shape of the hyoid bone, then you know the hyoid's position in the throat.

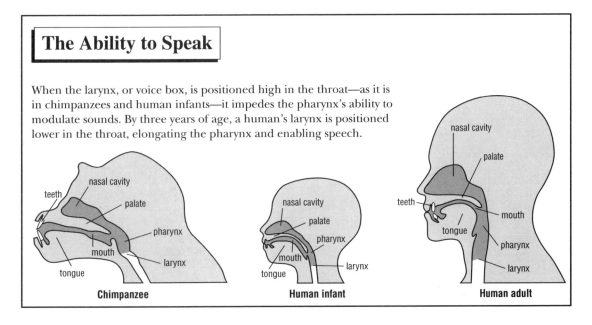

The Ability to Speak

When the larynx, or voice box, is positioned high in the throat—as it is in chimpanzees and human infants—it impedes the pharynx's ability to modulate sounds. By three years of age, a human's larynx is positioned lower in the throat, elongating the pharynx and enabling speech.

Chimpanzee

nasal cavity
teeth
palate
pharynx
mouth
larynx
tongue

Human infant

nasal cavity
palate
pharynx
mouth
larynx
tongue

Human adult

nasal cavity
palate
teeth
mouth
tongue
pharynx
larynx

And if you know the hyoid's position, then you know where the larynx is positioned, too. And in every major respect, this . . . man had a hyoid built just like ours today.[81]

Anthropologist Baruch Arensburg of Tel Aviv University believes that Neandertal burial practices support the theory that this species could talk.

The idea that Middle Paleolithic people were mute . . . is ridiculous. This person [who contributed the hyoid bone] was intentionally buried by his fellows. You cannot tell a gorilla to go bury his grandfather. You cannot learn abstract things through imitation. If people do not have language they do not have traditions. And if they have traditions, then they must have had language.[82]

Complex Society

Neandertal burials also suggest that this species might have known love and compassion. Some Neandertal skeletons represent the remains of elderly (for these people, age thirty) or sick individuals. Clearly the tribe cared for them, or they would not have survived.

Moreover, because the importance of these old or injured Neandertals was not due to their physical strength, some scientists suggest that their society valued individual contributions. Anthropologist Erik Trinkaus and scientist Pat Shipman, in their book *The Neandertals*, explain:

[One] indicator of strong social ties and social complexity [among Neandertals] is the survival of individuals with severe, sometimes crippling injuries; an individual's value was not solely based on his or her ability to obtain food or carry out physical work effectively. This fact . . . suggests that there was an elaboration of different roles within Neandertal society: different individuals did different things. Those who did not or could not procure food must have been supported by the rest of the group who valued their other contributions. Just what those contributions may have been—knowledge? art? music? linguistic gifts?—remains elusive.[83]

The idea that Neandertals recognized individuality might also be supported by the way they decorated their dead. Trinkaus and Shipman report that Neandertals sometimes made simple body ornaments and that these ornaments, as well as items placed around the body, "indicate that [the] social roles [of the deceased] were complex."[84] They explain individuality in burials:

Seemingly, the social role or status of an individual could be modified or signified through voluntary changes in personal appearance. In some sense, the ornaments an individual wore gave the message, "this is who or what I am"—meaning that not everyone was the same. What's more, an individual's standing continued to exist after death, long enough for his or her social group to bury the body. And burial often occurred in a specific, unnatural posture, showing that the corpse was not simply dropped into some convenient depression in the earth without preparation. A dead Neandertal was more than a dead animal or an inert lump: he or

Men and women gather to feast during a ceremony for a dead comrade. The evidence of Neandertal burials causes many scientists to conclude that Neandertals experienced love and compassion.

she was a specific person, about whom others cared. Individuality—the specialness of one person from any other—took on a meaning that did not seem to have previously existed in human evolution.[85]

Cannibalism?

Some scientists believe that this recognition of individuality explains Neandertal cannibalism. At a few archaeological sites, such as a rock shelter in Krapina, Yugoslavia, and a cave at the mouth of the Klasies River in Africa, there is evidence that early *Homo sapiens* heated human skulls, then broke them open to eat the cooked brains inside. This practice also occurred among *Homo erectus* in China. One explanation for such cannibalism is tribal ritual. As James Shreeve explains,

The belief systems of many tribal societies include ceremonial eating of selected parts of the deceased, in the

communal hope that some quality of the departed—his spirit, wisdom, strength—will thereby be passed on and preserved. The fierce Yanomamo Indians of the Amazon consume the ashes of their comrades who have been killed in raids. A pinch of Fallen Comrade is added to boiled plaintain soup at the funeral ceremony, and served up again whenever a revenge raid is in the offing. "This puts them into the appropriate stage of rage for the business of killing," writes anthropologist Napoleon Chagnon, who has spent many years with the Yanomamo.[86]

Shreeve believes that this kind of cannibalism "would seem to demonstrate a layered mental landscape, a sense that things—in this case, the ashes of a corpse—embody powers, values, or meanings beyond their physical [form]."[87] However, he says it is also possible that this cannibalism was a response to famine, pointing out that "eating your own kind merely to stay alive . . . demonstrates nothing but an extreme state of starvation."[88]

Disappearing Species

Whether or not Neandertals were cannibals is still a matter of debate. So is the question of why and how this species disappeared from earth between 50,000 and 35,000 years ago. Some scientists believe that Neandertals evolved into *Homo sapiens sapiens*, the subfamily that includes modern humans, while others believe that Neandertals became extinct.

New DNA research seems to support the idea of Neandertal extinction. In 1997 scientists extracted this genetic material from the first Neandertal bones ever discovered. They learned that the Neandertals of the Neander Valley in Germany did not pass on their DNA to modern humans.

However, Trinkaus and Shipman point out that Neandertal groups might have met different fates depending on where they lived. In other words, Neandertals might have become extinct in some regions, while evolving into early *Homo sapiens sapiens* in others. For example, they say that in parts of central Europe, "there is abundant evidence of continuous evolution, genetic admixture and interbreeding between the resident Neandertals and the early modern humans who were filtering in slowly from the Levant [in the Middle East] and possibly elsewhere."[89] They explain:

> Specific details in the shape of the nose and brows, and particular features of the back of the skull and the femur that are shared by Neandertals and modern humans in central Europe, all indicate genetic continuity during the long period over which a major anatomical change from fully Neandertal to fully modern human occurred.[90]

Trinkaus and Shipman believe that this evolutionary process was extremely gradual and took place alongside the extinction of some Neandertal tribes.

> The mosaic of local evolution, migration, admixture, absorption, or local extinction of Neandertals was a complex process that occurred over at least 10,000 years. This is a long time for modern humans to spread from the Levant to the Atlantic coast of Europe, whether or not Neandertals were "in the way." Slowly, the populations expanded, absorbed or displaced local inhabitants, developed new genetic and behavioral adaptations to new circumstances, retaining the best of the Neandertals and combining it with the emerging features of the newcomers who more closely resembled ourselves.[91]

Trinkaus and Shipman add that this extinction did not happen immediately, or at the same time in every region. Based on their studies of fossils in the Middle East, they say:

> To us, the fossils indicate that the earliest modern humans evolved out of Neandertals (or out of late archaic peoples very like them) soon after Neandertals had themselves appeared, about 100,000 years ago. This was not an evolutionary event that happened simultaneously across the entire Neandertal range. Africa has been a popular choice for the birthplace of early modern humans, but new dates on fossil sites from the Levant show that early modern humans were there as early as in Africa; the same has been suggested for some eastern Asian sites. . . . But the first ap-

pearance of the modern humans is not the same thing as the end of the Neandertals, at least in the Levant.[92]

No Interaction

In the Levant region, several sites have been discovered that indicate that Neandertals and early modern humans lived alongside one another. Scientists are still trying to discover whether, or how, these hominids interacted, but preliminary studies indicate that in this particular region they did not interbreed. James Shreeve believes this is because the two species' faces were very different:

Human mate-recognition systems are overwhelmingly visual. . . . The locus of the human body that lures, captures, and holds the eye most of all is the face. . . . This brings us back to the Levant: two human species in a tight space for a long time. The vortex of anatomy where Neandertals and early moderns differed most emphatically, where a clear line can be drawn between *them* and *us* . . . is the face.[93]

Shreeve suggests that Neandertals used faces to recognize tribe members and, consequently, prospective mates. He says that if this is true, then "their cohabitation with moderns in the Levant no longer needs explanation. The Neandertals and moderns managed to co-exist through those long millennia, doing the same humanlike things, but without interbreeding, simply because the issue never really came up."[94] In other words, these two groups of people just were not attracted to each other.

But Trinkaus and Shipman offer another reason why the two groups did not interact. They suggest that Neandertals migrated into the region during one part of the year, whereas the modern humans migrated there during another, saying:

We find it easier to envision that modern humans and Neandertals remained [apart]—and that they avoided coming into direct competition for resources— if the region were a fluctuating contact zone or boundary, with first one and then the other type of human occupying the area alternatively. This interpretation argues that the two groups appear to overlap in time and space only because of the familiar problems of the sparseness of the fossil record and the crudeness of our dating techniques.[95]

But regardless of the reason, Neandertals in the Levant remained a separate species, and none of their DNA survives today. Over time, early *Homo sapiens sapiens* supplanted *Homo neanderthalensis*, and eventually all Neandertals on earth were replaced by this species. *Homo sapiens sapiens* proved to be highly successful. It was clever and complex, creating many new behaviors and developing a more intricate social structure than its predecessors.

5 From Upper Paleolithic to Neolithic: *Homo Sapiens Sapiens*

The first modern humans, *Homo sapiens sapiens*, appeared in Africa between 200,000 and 50,000 years ago, in the Middle East about 100,000 years ago, in Australia 60,000 years ago, and in Europe 20,000 years ago. This coincided with the period of the Stone Age called the Upper Paleolithic, which occurred in the late Pleistocene Epoch of geologic history.

These new hominids lacked the projected facial features of the Neandertal, and their bodies were taller and less robust; in appearance, they were quite close to today's humans. Longer legs gave them the ability to travel longer distances, which meant that they came in contact with many other tribes of people. This exposure to other cultures and ideas may be the source of their greater creativity, in comparison to their ancestors.

Advances in Tool Technology

The best evidence for a new level of human creativity is related to tool technology. Archaeologists agree that early *Homo sapiens sapiens* made a wider variety of tools than archaic *Homo sapiens* or Neandertals and that it developed new uses for tools. Roger Lewin explains:

Between 250,000 and 150,000 years ago the pace of change of tool technologies began to accelerate. Whereas continuity was the hallmark of tool-making prior to this turning point, change began to dominate thereafter. Moreover, each succeeding culture contained a larger array of finer implements than the last. Bone, antler and ivory became increasingly important raw materials for tool-making, particularly for fine, flexible and sharp implements. And, most striking of all, there began to emerge a previously unseen degree of variability in the form of tool-kits [tool groupings] found in neighboring sites, a variability that has been explained [either] as [a slight difference in a tool's function] or cultural expression through style.[96]

Moreover, according to Richard Klein, early *Homo sapiens sapiens* began to develop tools whose prime function was to make other tools.

In general, late-Pleistocene artifact assemblages contain a much wider range of recognizable artifact types than do earlier ones, suggesting that late-Pleistocene people were engaged in a wider range of activities. These . . . included the manufacture of more tools for creation of other tools rather than for immediate use as hide scrapers, projectile points, etc.[97]

Klein also says that early *Homo sapiens sapiens* seemed to be making many tools that had to be pieced together. He explains:

To judge by the small size or the shape of many late-Pleistocene stone artifacts and by the form of many bone pieces, the people probably also manufactured many more composite tools, that is, implements combining separate pieces of stone, bone, or other materials. Unfortunately, because the composite tools were held together mainly by perishable glues, leather thongs, and so forth, few have survived to the present.[98]

The first major tool industry, or culture, of the *Homo sapiens sapiens* was the Mousterian. Approximately 34,000 years ago, during the Upper Paleolithic Period, this gave way to the Aurignacian and the Perigordian, which included a subindustry called the Gravettian. The Aurignacian culture existed until approximately 29,000 years ago, whereas the Perigordian existed until approximately 21,000 years ago, and the Gravettian until 17,000 years ago.

In certain parts of France and Spain, the Perigordian culture was followed by the Solutrean, which existed from approximately 20,000 to 16,000 years ago. The Solutrean culture featured blades carefully shaped like laurel leaves, as well as the first eyed sewing needles. It was followed by the Azilian culture, which existed from approximately 9,500 to 9,200 years ago.

In the remaining parts of Europe the Perigordian culture was followed by the

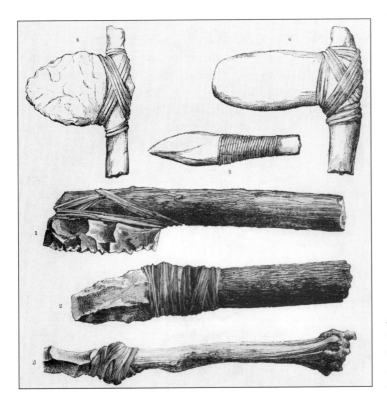

A diagram shows early flint weapons made by Homo sapiens sapiens *and their possible uses: 1) a saw, 2) a chisel, 3) a knife, 4) a flint ax, 5) a spear, and 6) a wooden ax.*

European Homo sapiens sapiens *are believed to have lived in huts constructed with animal bones, similar to this museum exhibit's modern recreation.*

Magdalenian, which existed from approximately 17,000 years ago to 9,000 years ago, during the Mesolithic Period. The Magdalenian was noted for its bows and arrows, and for its stone saws, which were used to make houses.

By this time, early *Homo sapiens sapiens* had learned to construct its own dwellings, rather than relying solely on natural homes such as caves and rock shelters. It used whatever materials were at hand. For example, in Africa it used poles and mud to build huts, whereas in Europe it used large animal bones and hides. Its houses also differed according to climate. African huts typically had an outside awning, to shade people from the heat; northern European huts were slightly subterranean, to shelter people from the arctic cold.

Cooperative Hunting

Advances in tools and housing were accompanied by more sophisticated hunting techniques. For example, birds were caught with snares and hunted with bows and arrows. Traps, spears, harpoons, and hooks were used to catch fish. By this time, people had discovered the dietary value of shellfish and other forms of mollusk.

In addition, scientists agree that *Homo sapiens sapiens* hunted cooperatively in order to kill larger and more dangerous game, including reindeer, large bison and antelope, horses, and wild boar. It also planned its hunts, following animals' migratory patterns as they moved from winter to summer feeding grounds.

However, scientists disagree about whether hominids ever hunted an ancient species called the woolly mammoth. Bones from this creature, which resembled a large elephant, have been found at an important *Homo sapiens sapiens* site in the former Czechoslovakia called the Dolni Vestonice.

Archaeologists believe that Dolni Vestonice was some kind of village. It had several dwellings, the largest of which was approximately fifty by thirty feet in size, and this group of dwellings was surrounded by a fence made of mammoth bones. Outside this fence were the remains of about a hundred additional mammoths. Therefore when the site was discovered, some scientists, including Bohuslav Klima of the Czech Institute of Archaeology, immediately concluded that the people of Dolni Vestonice hunted mammoths. James Shreeve explains:

[Klima] noted the location of the site, a few hundred meters above the river plain, where a sharp eye could monitor the passing of migrating herds of mammoth and other game; he noted the "vast accumulation" of mammoth bones piled up in the marsh, presumably the leavings of the hunters' meals, and pondered over other smashed-up mammoth bones on the site, some of which had been broken to extract their marrow, others bashed apart "in connection with various magical customs—seemingly to assure success in the hunt." The story he coaxed from all

this became the classic Ice Age tale: a large, cooperative community, drawn to this spot on the landscape specifically to hunt "the mighty pachyderm."[99]

However, Shreeve says that there is an alternative explanation for these bones:

If extinct mammoth behaved like their modern elephant cousins, when they grew old they migrated to marshy areas, where there would be softer vegetation for their worn teeth to chew. Eventually, the old would die. Over time their bones would be washed together in . . . swampy areas [like Dolni Vestonice] by the action of water flow. Mammoth bones make good building material, and if you can get a fire hot enough, excellent fuel too. [Archaeologist] Olga Soffer at the University of Illinois believes that people were drawn to this spot because there was a natural supply of fuel and building material available.[100]

Scientists disagree whether Homo sapiens sapiens *ever hunted woolly mammoths. Many experts believe that the mammoth bones found in fossil sites were scavenged by early humans after the animals had died of natural causes.*

According to Soffer, "The site has nothing to do with hunting. . . . If people were getting together, there must have been some kind of relationship among them. So I'd say Dolni Vestonice was some kind of kin aggregation site."[101]

Archaeological evidence shows that the people who lived at Dolni Vestonice had an intricate society that recognized the importance of family relationships. Scientists call these people Cro-Magnons, a name derived from the place where they were first discovered in 1868, a rock shelter called Cro-Magnon in a region of southwest France. At one time, the term *Cro-Magnon* was used to label all early modern humans, whereas now it is used to refer only to those who lived in Europe between approximately 34,000 and 10,000 years ago. All others living throughout the world prior to the Bronze Age are simply referred to as early *Homo sapiens sapiens*, or early modern humans.

Immovable Art

From fossils and artifacts, scientists have theorized that Cro-Magnons and other early *Homo sapiens sapiens* lived in family groups. In some places, these groups were small, whereas in others they were a great deal larger and more complicated. Richard Klein says that bigger groups were particularly likely among the Magdalenian culture of France and Spain, approximately 15,000 to 11,000 years ago. He explains:

*Re-creations of three prehistoric hominids—*Pithecanthropus, *Neandertal, and Cro-Magnon—show their similarities and differences.*

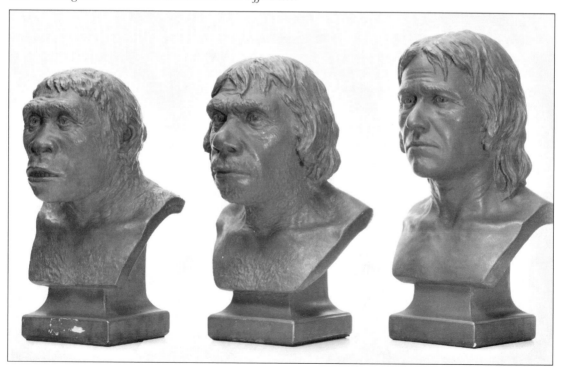

Some late-Pleistocene people inhabiting very rich settings that supported much denser populations may have lived in complex, "ranked" societies like those of the historic hunter-gatherers of the American Pacific Northwest. In this instance, a [group] of hereditary chiefs may have coordinated many activities, including food acquisition and distribution, rituals and ceremonies, trade, and even warfare.[102]

Early *Homo sapiens sapiens* left behind evidence of these rituals and ceremonies, not through its tools but through its artwork and burial practices. This evidence suggests that Middle and Late Stone Age people were similar to tribal cultures today. As Klein says, "The thoughts, ideas, beliefs, and values of late-Pleistocene people are not preserved in the archaeological record, but their art and their graves provide the first clear evidence for ideological systems like those of historic people."[103]

The artwork of early modern humans appears in two basic forms: as paintings or carvings on an immovable surface, such as a cave wall, and as portable sculptures or similar small objects. The earliest immovable art, created by Cro-Magnons between 34,000 and 12,000 years ago, appears in caves throughout France and Spain.

Three of the most spectacular examples of cave art occur at sites called Altamira, Lascaux, and Chauvet Cave. Altamira, in northeast Spain, was discovered in 1879 by landowner Don Marcelino de Sautuola and his twelve-year-old daughter. This cave has approximately twenty-five painted animals on its ceiling. According to Tom Prideaux,

Some were life-sized, or even larger, and in the wavering lamplight they seemed to pulse with life. Colored in rich browns, reds, yellows and black, they sometimes conformed to the shape of the rock itself; the artist had purposely positioned them to take advantage of the Altamira ceiling's undulating contours. A rounded haunch, for example, was painted over a protuberance in the stone, thus creating a three-dimensional effect that was uncannily realistic.[104]

The second site, Lascaux, was discovered by four boys looking for their dog in the Dordogne region of France in 1940. The dog had fallen into a hole made by an uprooted tree, and when one of the boys crawled down after it, he found a cave whose walls had been elaborately painted. According to Prideaux's comparison with the art at Altamira:

[The paintings at Lascaux] are much less tranquil and much more variegated. . . . Where Altamira's animals, for the most part, are relaxed and stately, the Lascaux beasts are often running wild; one famous rendering, known as the falling horse, is head-over-hoofs upside down. Where the Altamira artists had a firm control of color and movement, the Lascaux painters applied pigments loosely and used wavy lines that are almost baroque in their swirl and dash. Where Altamira appears classic and orthodox, Lascaux is freewheeling and, to modern viewers, exotic.[105]

These paintings are estimated to be approximately 17,000 years old. There are several of them, and they appear not only in the main cavern but also in several side chambers, along with rock carvings and unusual symbols that might have been a form of writing. The main cavern has also been called the "Great Hall of Bulls" because it has a large frieze dominated by bulls; other animals also appear in this frieze, including a two-horned, horselike creature that many scientists consider to be a mythical beast similar to a unicorn.

The Chauvet Cave, discovered in southern France in 1994, is still being explored and studied. Scientists estimate that it is approximately 31,000 years old and has at least five underground chambers. The site features paintings of over three hundred different types of animals, styled similarly to those at Lascaux.

This early immovable art typically features animals and hunting scenes. As Jean McMann says in her book *Riddles of the Stone Age*, these works "seem to have served

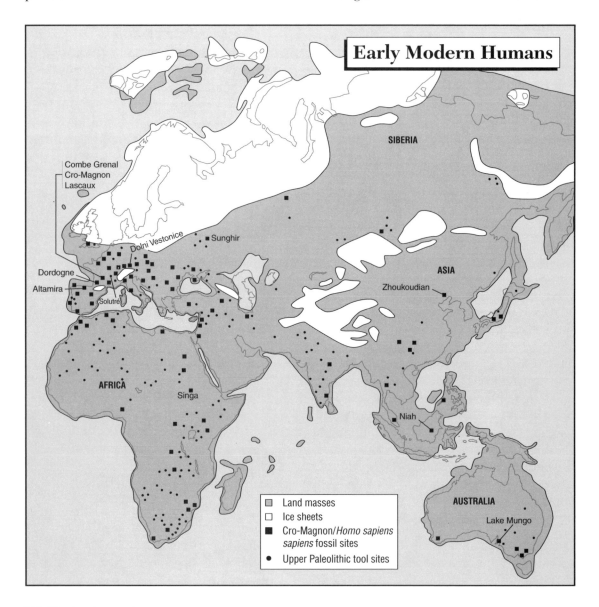

Early Modern Humans

SIBERIA

Combe Grenal
Cro-Magnon
Lascaux

Dolni Vestonice

Sunghir

ASIA

Zhoukoudian

Dordogne

Altamira

Solutré

AFRICA

Singa

Niah

AUSTRALIA

Lake Mungo

☐ Land masses
☐ Ice sheets
■ Cro-Magnon/*Homo sapiens sapiens* fossil sites
• Upper Paleolithic tool sites

A scene from the caves at Lascaux, France. Scientists believe these figures were drawn by Stone Age artists.

as hunting magic, yet the artists show affection for the animals as well as pleasure in the act of painting itself."[106] However, there are still some mysteries regarding the animal subjects of these paintings. As Richard Leakey explains,

> The most common animal depicted in the caves is the horse, followed by the bison and the ox. These three animals make up 60% of all the animal images. Deer, mammoth, ibex, reindeer, antelope, wild goat, wild boar, rhino, lion, hyaena, fox and wolf are occasionally found but are much less common, while birds and fish are very rare. Strangely enough, the bones found in caves where people lived tell us that reindeer and ibexes were very important food items to these artists. So why did they paint them so rarely?[107]

In addition, while human handprints are a common feature in cave art, entire human figures are not. Richard Leakey finds this puzzling, saying:

Even more surprising is the scarcity of human images. The few that are found are only very sketchy outlines. If animals could be drawn in such detail then why not humans? Presumably there was some sort of superstition prohibiting the depiction of human beings.[108]

Leakey adds that in some caves, human heads are depicted on animal bodies. One such figure, which scientists have named "The Sorcerer," has a deer's antlers and ears, a horse's body and tail, but human legs and feet, as well as a long beard like that of a man. Leakey notes that it is "carved on a rather inaccessible part of the cave 4 metres (13 feet) above the floor. Beneath 'The Sorcerer' are hundreds of engraved animals but only 'The Sorcerer' is outlined in black paint."[109] Leakey believes that this and other aspects of cave art indicate that these places were "associated with some sort of ritual. It is found in inaccessible places in the depths of caves, there are no detailed

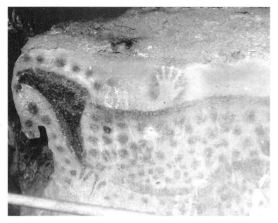

A human handprint is visible in this painting from the Stone Age.

human figures, and many of the animals depicted were not normally hunted. . . . All these things suggest that cave art had some sort of mystical significance."[110]

Scientists will never be completely certain about the meanings behind cave art. Similarly, they do not understand why this artwork changed so drastically over time. Later artists did not feature animals in their immovable art, as Cro-Magnons had. McMann says:

> During the Neolithic, or Late Stone Age (from 5000 to 2000 BC in Europe), the realistic and often light-hearted representations of hunters and animals disappear. The art becomes abstract. Spirals and geometric designs appear on stones and rock surfaces, sometimes executed with great care and finesse, at other times hastily scratched—like a doodle. Many are inscribed on single stones standing or lying in fields, usually near the sea. Others are carved on stone temples and burial structures.[111]

McMann says that no one knows the reason for these ornamented stones, or *megaliths*, which occur in the British Isles, Scandinavia, Germany, France, Spain, Portugal, and Malta. However, scientists have speculated that some might have been related to religious beliefs. McMann explains:

> The presence of human remains together with other clues in the European megaliths implies that their function had to do with ideas about death—that they were constructed out of love or fear of the "ghosts" or souls of departed ancestors. Other sites, such as those in Malta, show no sign of being built for burial.[112]

Grave Sites

Wherever grave sites are found, scientists often discover various types of portable art, also called *art mobilier*. These carved and engraved items, typically made of bone or ivory, are as intricate as cave art. Roger Lewin explains:

> Many art mobilier objects are decorated with geometric patterns; some have pictures of animals, fish and plants; and others have series of seemingly random notches. Alexander Marshack's detailed studies of such objects reveals something more coherent to this aspect of prehistoric art than has previously been supposed. For example, he interprets the images of a male and female seal, a male salmon, two coiled snakes and a flower in bloom, all engraved on a baton made from reindeer antler, as a representation of Spring. Other apparently jumbled images engraved on

ivory knives, flaking tools and the like can be similarly interpreted as seasonal vignettes.[113]

The most common forms of *art mobilier* are small, carved objects and figurines. While scientists cannot be sure what functions they were intended to fulfill, some theories have been proposed. Richard Klein reports:

> Some engraved . . . objects that are otherwise enigmatic may have been gaming pieces, while others were perhaps counting or recording devices, even lunar calendars. Many animal figurines could be . . . symbols of kinship groups, while the human figurines could obviously represent deities or spirits. Most are highly stylized, lacking facial features or details of the hands and feet. Many, known popularly as "Venus figurines," have exaggerated buttocks and breasts, leading to speculation that they were fertility symbols or depictions of earth-mother goddesses.[114]

These objects were often buried alongside dead tribal members, sometimes in individual graves and sometimes in pits that held several bodies. Early *Homo sapiens sapiens* were the first hominids to practice multiple burial. There are many examples of this, but one of the best known was discovered recently at Dolni Vestonice, where three teenagers were buried together. Believed to be a woman in between two men, the skeletons were carefully posed. According to James Shreeve,

"The Sorcerer," an imaginative drawing that combines the physical characteristics of a deer, a horse, and a human, may have been drawn for use in an ancient ritual.

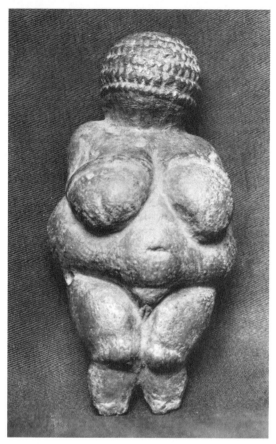

A Venus figurine shows the exaggerated physical features thought to symbolize fertility.

The most peculiar feature of the grave . . . was the arrangement of the deceased. Whoever committed the bodies to the ground extended them side by side, the woman between her two companions. The man on her left lay on his stomach, facing away from her but with his left arm linked with hers. The other male lay on his back, his head turned toward her. Both of his arms were reaching out, so that his hands rested on her pubis. The ground surrounding this intimate connection was splashed with red ocher [pigment derived from clay].[115]

This red coloring also appeared on all three skulls. In addition, the bodies of the two men had been ornamented with necklaces. Such ornamentation also appears at other multiple burial sites. In his book *Cro-Magnon Man*, Tom Prideaux describes one grave, estimated to be approximately 22,000 years old, that was discovered near Moscow, Russia, in 1969:

> The skeletons of two boys [were] both on their backs, their legs pointing in opposite directions, their skulls almost touching. Head to head, they stretched out in one line. The younger boy was somewhere between seven and nine, the other about five years older. Besides their lavishly beaded garments, they were equipped with weapons, including eight-foot-long spears, made from straightened mammoth tusks, with very sharp, thin points. Both corpses wore ivory bracelets and rings, and there was evidence of headgear of some sort; long pins under their chins had been used for fastening the collars of their garments to keep them warm and snug.[116]

Richard Klein agrees that "the beads and other objects found with the skeletons were apparently sewn on the clothing as decorations or fasteners."[117] He believes that sewing was accomplished using bones as needles and leather strips or sinew as thread. He also reports that these clothes were relatively "sophisticated" and "well-tailored," and "suggest the details of fur or leather dress, comprising a cap, a shirt, a jacket, trousers, and moccasins."[118]

These elaborate clothes and the possessions that surrounded them tell a lot about early modern humans. While Neandertals sometimes placed a few items near the deceased, their graves did not approach this level of decoration; scientists therefore disagree about the thought processes behind the funeral practices of these two species. In any event, the graves of early *Homo sapiens sapiens* leave no doubt that these people viewed death in a highly complex way. As Prideaux explains,

An illustration depicts the skeletal remains of a human buried in Paleolithic times at Sunghir, Russia. The head and chest of the skeleton are decorated with ivory beads that apparently had been sewn onto cloth.

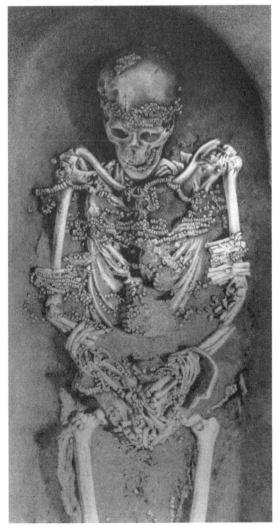

No one knows whether all these [accessories] were to provide status for the boys in afterlife, or to warm and comfort their souls, or simply to honor the family's important position in earthly society. But whatever their purpose, they were clearly symbolic; the objects stood, in the eyes of the people who put them there, for something else, something that was important enough to expend a considerable amount of worldly wealth on. This is a practice that has claimed a good deal of man's energy and riches in the millennia since.[119]

In addition to respecting the dead, early *Homo sapiens sapiens* placed a high value on human life. It appears that members of the species rarely killed one another, either through murder or warfare. Richard Klein reports that "skeletal evidence for deliberate injury is . . . rare, probably because, like most . . . hunter-gatherers, late-Pleistocene ones rarely engaged in warfare or interpersonal violence."[120] However, he adds that "although violence is rare, it does exist"[121] and cites a few instances where individuals were clearly killed by stone knives or spearheads.

Interestingly, Klein also describes a situation where early modern humans probably attempted to heal a sick individual. Scientists studying a Magdalenian site in France discovered the skeleton of a child whose skull showed the classic symptoms of hydrocephaly. In this fatal condition, cerebrospinal fluid swells in the brain and causes the forehead to bulge outward. Klein reports that this skull had "an artificial perforation that was probably intended to relieve the condition."[122]

Scientists do not know whether early *Homo sapiens sapiens* practiced other forms of medicine. However, they do know that these people were generally healthier than their predecessors. Klein says, "Maximum life expectancy probably exceeded that of the Neanderthals, perhaps by as much as 20%. As a consequence, late-Pleistocene human groups probably contained more older people, whose accumulated knowledge could promote group survival, particularly in times of crisis."[123] The maximum life expectancy for men was fifty or sixty years old; however, for women it was only forty, because many died in childbirth.

As people began living longer, the overall population of *Homo sapiens sapiens* increased. No one knows exactly how many men and women existed during the late Pleistocene Epoch; however, according to Richard Klein, scientists do know that by the beginning of the Neolithic Period, there were humans in all parts of the world. He reports that "late-Pleistocene people greatly extended the geographic range of humankind by colonizing easternmost Europe, Siberia, the Americas, and Australia."[124]

Travel and Language

This colonization was accomplished primarily during the Mesolithic Period, which began at the end of the last Ice Age, also called the Wurm/Wisconsin glaciation, approximately 10,000 years ago. The term *Mesolithic* refers only to European history, although some scientists also use it to refer to the global transition from Old to New Stone Age. It was a time of increased transportation, when people created boats, sleds, and skis, yet it was marked by an unstable geography.

After the last Ice Age, the earth's temperatures fluctuated between warm and cold cycles. Glaciers shifted accordingly, and sea levels rose and fell. In addition, volcanic activity resulted in the obliteration of all life-forms in some areas and the sudden upthrusting of dry land in others. Thus, landmasses were variably covered and uncovered, and populations were able to walk or canoe into new areas. Eventually the climate stabilized and grew warmer, and the glaciers permanently receded. This allowed Mesolithic people to exploit even broader areas for settlement. Therefore, Phillip Van Doren Stern says:

> Perhaps the most important thing accomplished by Mesolithic people was their pushing on to new frontiers. Since they lived at a time when the retreat of the glacier was making more land available, they settled northern Europe. The population of the British Isles, which had been so small, now began to increase. . . . Scandinavia also began to be settled, although a few deer bones, broken open to get at the marrow, indicate that man may have entered Denmark at an earlier period.[125]

In addition, Stern credits Mesolithic people with being the first to domesticate the dog. Otherwise, he says, their culture was much like that of Upper Paleolithic people.

However, their widespread colonization coincided with an explosion of language. Scientists do not doubt that early modern humans were capable of complex communication. In fact, according to Richard Leakey and Roger Lewin, "After perhaps 100,000 years, some five thousand languages existed, the number documented in recent historic times. Five thou-

A Mesolithic family group is depicted with many of the accoutrements associated with them, including a boat (left) and a domesticated dog.

sand languages, each rooted through complex evolutionary relationship to an original mother tongue."[126]

As people became isolated by language as well as distance, their cultures became more distinct. Therefore, Leakey and Lewin conclude:

> Ironically, the cognitive ability that unifies all of *Homo sapiens* also fragments *Homo sapiens*. For five thousand languages means five thousand cultures,

each a social and spiritual milieu that differentiates and, all too often, separates one from another.[127]

Agriculture

The Neolithic Period, which marks the end of the Stone Age and lasted from approximately 10,000 B.C. to the beginning of the Bronze Age (about 3500 B.C.), was therefore characterized by a new level of diversity among human beings. However, some generalizations can be made about this period.

With the onset of the Neolithic, the glaciers receded and global temperatures warmed. Consequently, the amount of edible vegetation increased. At the same time, a warmer climate meant that people required less meat, which has a relatively high concentration of fat and calories. A diet rich in meat helps the human body survive lower temperatures, but once the climate was no longer so cold, people could eat more plants and berries. It was a short step from gathering to cultivating and harvesting. In fact, the beginning of agriculture is one of the defining features of the Neolithic Period.

However, there is another reason for the onset of agriculture besides climate. Roger Lewin reports:

The postglacial period must indeed have brought substantial environmental changes, but, argues Mark Cohen of the State University of New York, similar changes had occurred in earlier times, so what was special about the shift 10,000 years ago? Population pressure is the answer. Population growth over the millennia, since the emergence of modern humans, had eventually reached a point at which local groups were finding it difficult to obtain sufficient food from hunting and gathering, which requires people to live in groups of about 25 individuals and each group to have access to at least 75 km [kilometers of land]. As a result, people began to nurture their own food crops and control livestock,

thus allowing a higher population density in any given area.[128]

Emerging Trade

Other scientists support a different reason for the development of agriculture. They believe that the portable artwork of early modern humans was used in trade and suggest that agricultural products could have been traded as well. For example, Lewin cites the belief of British anthropologist Barbara Bender that some late Stone Age people acquired extra food specifically for trading purposes:

Hunting and gathering societies were becoming more and more complex and hierarchical, [Bender] says, as indicated by the appearance of trade items and status burials long before the Agricultural Revolution occurred. The elaboration of alliances and trade between neighbouring groups would have generated pressure to produce more and more surplus goods, which eventually would have been most efficiently served by a sedentary economy.[129]

But whatever the reason for the development of agriculture, along with it came new behaviors. People experimented with different types of cultivation and created even more tools, such as the sickle, as well as larger equipment, such as the plow and the wheel. Moreover, as agriculturalists, Neolithic people had to live primarily in one place. Therefore they built villages, stopped following animal migration patterns, and began raising animals for food.

Their most important domestic animals were cattle, goat, sheep, and, in the late Neolithic Period, pigs. They also kept horses, not for eating but for transportation and as working animals, which they trained to perform a variety of useful tasks.

In many regions, they started using wood to construct their homes, and chopping down trees gave them even more land to cultivate. They also used the "slash and burn" method to acquire more land, setting brush on fire to clear it away. They used this bare land to grow wheat and other grains, which enabled them to create cereals as well as various legumes and oil crops such as linseed. They also continued to gather nuts and berries.

As their society became more settled, Neolithic people also became more inventive. In addition to their crops, tools, and farming equipment, they created elaborate basketry, pottery and the potter's wheel, and woven cloth. In fact, Stern says, "practically all of the world's primary inventions had been made by Neolithic times. Only metal remained to be discovered as a better material than stone for making implements and tools." [130]

At the same time, their cultures became more complex, basically indistinguishable from some tribal cultures still on earth today. As Ian Tattersall explains, "Around the world, societies have existed within our own century that employ (or employed) virtually all the technologies and economic strategies that have been developed since the beginning of the Upper Paleolithic." [131] By the end of the Stone Age, *Homo sapiens sapiens* had truly become the modern human.

Human Evolution

The Stone Age was a remarkable period in human history. At its beginning, early hominids were creatures who looked and lived much like apes, and their brains were clearly incapable of complex thought. But by the time the Stone Age gave way to the Bronze Age, Earth was populated with intelligent, creative human beings who thrived in complex societies. No longer scavengers forced to survive moment to moment, humans had developed planning behaviors that enabled them to cultivate their own food and even consider that there might be life after death.

Clearly, then, the greatest legacy of the Stone Age concerns the evolution of the human brain. While scientists disagree about how this evolution took place, they know where it led. As William Allman says, "With their explosion of culture, our ancient ancestors created a new social structure that drastically changed the way they went about their lives. In doing so, they set the human species on a trajectory that was to [continue for] thousands of years."[132]

But what does this say about the future of humanity? From what they know about human evolution in the past, scientists can

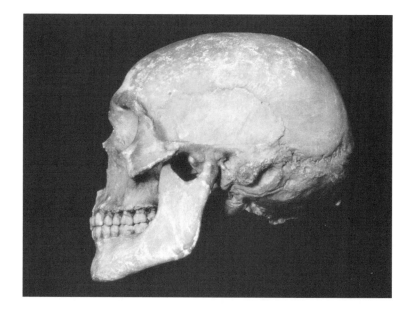

The skull of Homo sapiens, *an anatomically modern human. Scientists ponder whether humans will continue to evolve into more advanced species.*

extrapolate certain facts about the future. Scientist John Shea explains:

> At some point the . . . [physical] features and genes that are within the modern human population will cease to occur. Every other species that we find in the fossil record has a limited span of time. That's not to say we won't have descendants, who will take some other form, but that will depend on the context in which those evolutionary changes occur. But one knows that evolution will continue.[133]

Perhaps humans will have a new physical form, or their brains will evolve to offer them new insights and behaviors. Unforeseen geological events, such as our ancestors faced with the waxing and waning of the Ice Age, might also affect our future evolution. So might man-made eco-logical catastrophes. The lesson of the Stone Age is that change is inevitable. But whatever occurs, human beings have proved themselves capable of facing it. As Allman concludes:

> The human saga is a dynamic, ever changing process. . . . Our species has been constantly negotiating its place in Nature, reinventing itself and its behavior to adapt to an ever changing world. We continue to face new challenges, brought about by the technology of war, the potential for climate change, and the pressures of a growing population. Yet in some respects these challenges are no less daunting than those faced by our ancient ancestors on the savanna millions of years ago. They survived by inventing the future. Our task is nothing less.[134]

Notes

Introduction: The First Humans

1. Robert Lee Hotz, "Ancient Climate Changes Linked to Human Evolution," *Los Angeles Times*, October 6, 1995, home edition.

2. Quoted in Rod Caird, *Ape Man: The Story of Human Evolution*. New York: Macmillan, 1994, pp. 56–57.

3. Quoted in Phillip Van Doren Stern, *Prehistoric Europe: From Stone Age Man to the Early Greeks*. New York: W. W. Norton, 1969, p. 20.

4. Caird, *Ape Man*, p. 59.

5. Caird, *Ape Man*, p. 84.

Chapter 1: Classifying Prehistory

6. Jane McIntosh, *The Practical Archaeologist*. London: Facts On File, 1986, p. 10.

7. John Reader, *Missing Links: The Hunt for Earliest Man*. New York: Penguin Books, 1981, p. 17.

8. Reader, *Missing Links*, pp. 17–18.

9. Brian M. Fagan, *In the Beginning: An Introduction to Archaeology*. Boston: Little, Brown, 1978, pp. 95–96.

10. Ian Tattersall, *The Fossil Trail*. New York and Oxford: Oxford University Press, 1995, p. 8.

11. Tattersall, *The Fossil Trail*, p. 9.

12. McIntosh, *The Practical Archaeologist*, p. 14.

13. McIntosh, *The Practical Archaeologist*, p. 14.

14. Quoted in Reader, *Missing Links*, p. 5.

15. Reader, *Missing Links*, p. 1.

16. Reader, *Missing Links*, p. 6.

17. Reader, *Missing Links*, pp. 6–7.

18. Reader, *Missing Links*, p. 2.

19. Fagan, *In the Beginning*, p. 99.

20. Klein, *The Human Career: Human Biological and Cultural Origins*. Chicago and London: The University of Chicago Press, 1989, pp. 4–5.

21. Klein, *The Human Career*, p. 5.

22. Klein, *The Human Career*, p. 5.

23. Reader, *Missing Links*, p. 2.

24. Reader, *Missing Links*, p. 61.

25. Reader, *Missing Links*, p. 70.

26. Reader, *Missing Links*, p. 78.

Chapter 2: In the Beginning: Australopithecus *and* Homo Habilis

27. Klein, *The Human Career*, p. 103.

28. Klein, *The Human Career*, p. 106.

29. Klein, *The Human Career*, p. 106.

30. Klein, *The Human Career*, p. 106.

31. Donald Johanson and Maitland Edey, *Lucy: The Beginnings of Humankind*. New York: Warner Books, 1981, p. 18.

32. Caird, *Ape Man*, p. 112.

33. Caird, *Ape Man*, p. 115.

34. Caird, *Ape Man*, p. 44.

35. Caird, *Ape Man*, p. 44.

36. Caird, *Ape Man*, p. 44.

37. Caird, *Ape Man*, p. 48.

38. Reader, *Missing Links*, pp. 137–38.

39. Francis Clark Howell, *Early Man*. New York: Time Life Books, 1976, p. 53.

40. Klein, *The Human Career*, p. 167.

41. Howell, *Early Man*, p. 54.

42. Klein, *The Human Career*, p. 169.

43. Klein, *The Human Career*, p. 169.

44. Klein, *The Human Career*, p. 170.

45. Klein, *The Human Career*, p. 158.

46. Klein, *The Human Career*, p. 168.

47. Klein, *The Human Career*, p. 172.

Chapter 3: The Lower Paleolithic Period: Homo Erectus

48. Reader, *Missing Links*, p. 38.

49. Reader, *Missing Links*, p. 43.

50. Richard Leakey and Roger Lewin, *Origins*

Reconsidered: In Search of What Makes Us Human. New York: Doubleday, 1992, pp. 54–55.

51. Reader, *Missing Links*, pp. 46–47.

52. Klein, *The Human Career*, p. 183.

53. Quoted in Caird, *Ape Man*, p. 120.

54. Klein, *The Human Career*, p. 218.

55. Roger Lewin, *Human Evolution: An Illustrated Introduction.* New York: W. H. Freeman, 1984, pp. 23–24.

56. Klein, *The Human Career*, p. 222.

57. Quoted in Caird, *Ape Man*, p. 105.

58. Quoted in Caird, *Ape Man*, p. 105.

59. Klein, *The Human Career*, p. 427.

Chapter 4: The Middle Paleolithic Period: Archaic Homo Sapiens and Neandertal Man

60. Klein, *The Human Career*, p. 406.

61. Quoted in Rick Gore, "The First Europeans," *National Geographic*, vol. 192, no. 1, July 1997, p. 109.

62. Quoted in Gore, "The First Europeans," p. 109.

63. Richard E. Leakey, *Human Origins.* New York: Dutton, 1982, p. 57.

64. Leakey, *Human Origins*, p. 57.

65. Leakey, *Human Origins*, p. 57.

66. Klein, *The Human Career*, p. 408.

67. James Shreeve, *The Neandertal Enigma.* New York: Avon Books, 1995, p. 304.

68. Quoted in Shreeve, *The Neandertal Enigma*, p. 303.

69. Shreeve, *The Neandertal Enigma*, p. 135.

70. Shreeve, *The Neandertal Enigma*, p. 154.

71. Shreeve, *The Neandertal Enigma*, p. 155.

72. Shreeve, *The Neandertal Enigma*, p. 160.

73. Shreeve, *The Neandertal Enigma*, p. 261.

74. Shreeve, *The Neandertal Enigma*, p. 262.

75. George Constable, *The Neanderthals.* New York: Time Life Books, 1973, p. 75.

76. Shreeve, *The Neandertal Enigma*, p. 163.

77. Shreeve, *The Neandertal Enigma*, p. 164.

78. Shreeve, *The Neandertal Enigma*, p. 164.

79. Quoted in Shreeve, *The Neandertal Enigma*, p. 165.

80. Quoted in Gore, "The First Europeans," p. 109.

81. Quoted in Shreeve, *The Neandertal Enigma*, p. 190.

82. Quoted in Shreeve, *The Neandertal Enigma*, p. 190.

83. Erik Trinkaus and Pat Shipman, *The Neandertals.* New York: Vintage Books, 1992, p. 418.

84. Trinkaus and Shipman, *The Neandertals*, p. 418.

85. Trinkaus and Shipman, *The Neandertals*, p. 418.

86. Shreeve, *The Neandertal Enigma*, p. 230.

87. Shreeve, *The Neandertal Enigma*, p. 230.

88. Shreeve, *The Neandertal Enigma*, p. 230.

89. Trinkaus and Shipman, *The Neandertals*, p. 415.

90. Trinkaus and Shipman, *The Neandertals*, p. 415.

91. Trinkaus and Shipman, *The Neandertals*, p. 416.

92. Trinkaus and Shipman, *The Neandertals*, p. 414.

93. Shreeve, *The Neandertal Enigma*, p. 204.

94. Shreeve, *The Neandertal Enigma*, pp. 205–206.

95. Trinkaus and Shipman, *The Neandertals*, p. 415.

Chapter 5: From Upper Paleolithic to Neolithic: Homo Sapiens Sapiens

96. Lewin, *Human Evolution*, p. 67.

97. Klein, *The Human Career*, p. 369.

98. Klein, *The Human Career*, p. 369.

99. Shreeve, *The Neandertal Enigma*, p. 278.

100. Shreeve, *The Neandertal Enigma*, pp. 278–79.

101. Quoted in Shreeve, *The Neandertal Enigma*, p. 279.

102. Klein, *The Human Career*, p. 378.

103. Klein, *The Human Career*, p. 378.

104. Tom Prideaux, *Cro-Magnon Man*. New York: Time Life Books, 1973, pp. 93–94.

105. Prideaux, *Cro-Magnon Man*, p. 108.

106. Jean McMann, *Riddles of the Stone Age*. London: Thames and Hudson, 1980, p. 11.

107. Leakey, *Human Origins*, p. 65.

108. Leakey, *Human Origins*, pp. 65–66.

109. Leakey, *Human Origins*, p. 66.

110. Leakey, *Human Origins*, p. 66.

111. McMann, *Riddles of the Stone Age*, p. 11.

112. McMann, *Riddles of the Stone Age*, p. 12.

113. Lewin, *Human Evolution*, p. 90.

114. Klein, *The Human Career*, p. 382.

115. Shreeve, *The Neandertal Enigma*, pp. 265–66.

116. Prideaux, *Cro-Magnon Man*, p. 142.

117. Klein, *The Human Career*, pp. 370–71.

118. Klein, *The Human Career*, p. 370.

119. Prideaux, *Cro-Magnon Man*, p. 142.

120. Klein, *The Human Career*, p. 386.

121. Klein, *The Human Career*, p. 387.

122. Klein, *The Human Career*, p. 386.

123. Klein, *The Human Career*, p. 385.

124. Klein, *The Human Career*, p. 387.

125. Stern, *Prehistoric Europe*, p. 202.

126. Leakey and Lewin, *Origins Reconsidered*, pp. 274–75.

127. Leakey and Lewin, *Origins Reconsidered*, p. 275.

128. Lewin, *Human Evolution*, p. 95.

129. Quoted in Lewin, *Human Evolution*, p. 95.

130. Stern, *Prehistoric Europe*, p. 246.

131. Tattersall, *The Fossil Trail*, p. 246.

Epilogue: Human Evolution

132. William F. Allman, *The Stone Age Present*. New York: Touchstone, 1994, p. 218.

133. Quoted in Caird, *Ape Man*, p. 170.

134. Allman, *The Stone Age Present*, p. 254.

For Further Reading

Roger Lewin, *Bones of Contention*. New York: Simon and Schuster, 1987. For more advanced readers, this book by a scientist and journalist discusses many of the archaeological controversies involved in Stone Age history and culture.

Hazel Martell, *Over 6,000 Years Ago in the Stone Age*. New York: New Discovery Books/Macmillan, 1992. Clear and concise, this easy-to-read book gives basic information about the late Stone Age.

Anthony Mason, *The Time Trekkers Visit the Stone Age*. Brookfield, CT: Copper Beech Books, 1996. Designed for less advanced readers, this book is notable for its clever format, which takes time travelers back to early human history.

Nick Merriman, *Early Humans*. New York: Knopf (Eyewitness Books), 1989. This book has excellent photographs and illustrations related to Stone Age history and culture.

John E. Pfeiffer, *The Search for Early Man*. New York: Horizon Books, 1968. This book for young people provides the basic history of early fossil discoveries.

Konrad Spindler, *The Man in the Ice*. New York: Crown, 1994. This fascinating book for more advanced readers has many fine photographs and details the discovery of a 5,300-year-old body, indicating what it revealed about the late Stone Age.

Works Consulted

William F. Allman, *The Stone Age Present.* New York: Touchstone, 1994. By comparing modern human thinking and behavior to Stone Age thinking and behavior, this book makes some interesting assumptions about how evolution has influenced the people of today.

Rod Caird, *Ape Man: The Story of Human Evolution.* New York: Macmillan, 1994. Beautifully illustrated, this oversize book offers a great deal of current information about the Stone Age, including many quotes from prominent scientists.

George Constable, *The Neanderthals.* New York: Time Life Books, 1973. The text is somewhat outdated, but the illustrations and photographs concerning Neandertal fossil and artifact discovery are excellent.

Brian M. Fagan, *In the Beginning: An Introduction to Archaeology.* Boston: Little, Brown, 1978. This high school–level textbook provides a general discussion of archaeological study and early human behavior.

Rick Gore, "The First Europeans," *National Geographic*, vol. 192, no. 1, July 1997. Part of a series on early humans, this article gives current information about early *Homo sapiens sapiens* archaeological sites and research.

Robert Lee Hotz, "Ancient Climate Changes Linked to Human Evolution," *Los Angeles Times*, October 6, 1995, home edition. This article discusses current scientific thinking regarding the role of climate in the series of adaptive changes that culminated in modern humans.

Francis Clark Howell, *Early Man.* New York: Time Life Books, 1976. While its text is somewhat outdated, this book still offers excellent photographs and drawings concerning early Stone Age life and explains how important fossils and artifacts were discovered.

Donald Johanson and Maitland Edey, *Lucy: The Beginnings of Humankind.* New York: Warner Books, 1981. This book by one of the archaeologists present when the skeleton named "Lucy" was discovered offers details about that discovery and talks about early hominid life on earth.

Richard G. Klein, *The Human Career: Human Biological and Cultural Origins.* Chicago and London: The University of Chicago Press, 1989. This college-level textbook offers extensive details about all aspects of early human archaeology.

Richard E. Leakey, *Human Origins.* New York: Dutton, 1982. Designed for young adults and written by a leading archaeologist, this book offers an extremely clear discussion of human evolution.

Richard Leakey and Roger Lewin, *Origins Reconsidered: In Search of What Makes Us Human.* New York: Doubleday, 1992. Written by noted archaeologists, this book talks about important archaeological discoveries and the history of human evolution.

Roger Lewin, *Human Evolution: An Illustrated Introduction.* New York: W. H. Freeman, 1984. This book presents clear information about early humans and has many fine charts and graphs.

Jane McIntosh, *The Practical Archaeologist.* London: Facts On File, 1986. With many excellent illustrations and clearly written text, this book discusses human prehistory as well as the field of archaeology.

Jean McMann, *Riddles of the Stone Age.* London: Thames and Hudson, 1980. This book deals exclusively with Stone Age rock carvings in Europe; it presents many extremely detailed black-and-white photographs of their markings.

Douglas Preston, "The Lost Man," *The New Yorker,* June 16, 1997. This article, which describes the discovery of Neolithic fossils in Washington State, also discusses Stone Age tool technology.

Tom Prideaux, *Cro-Magnon Man.* New York: Time Life Books, 1973. Although somewhat outdated, this book presents valid information about the history of Cro-Magnon fossil and artifact discovery. In addition, it has many excellent photographs and detailed analyses of cave art.

John Reader, *Missing Links: The Hunt for Earliest Man.* New York: Penguin Books, 1981. Written by a journalist who specializes in science issues, this book is for readers interested in facts, dates, and basic information regarding the history of fossil discoveries and controversies.

James Shreeve, *The Neandertal Enigma.* New York: Avon Books, 1995. This book gives an extremely clear explanation of the current thinking regarding Neandertal evolution and behavior.

Phillip Van Doren Stern, *Prehistoric Europe: From Stone Age Man to the Early Greeks.* New York: W. W. Norton, 1969. This clearly written book traces the development of human culture in ancient Europe.

Ian Tattersall, *The Fossil Trail.* New York and Oxford: Oxford University Press, 1995. For more advanced readers, this book discusses fossil discoveries and archaeological controversies related to research on early hominids and human evolution.

Erik Trinkaus and Pat Shipman, *The Neandertals.* New York: Vintage Books, 1992. This book for more advanced readers traces the complete history of Neandertal fossil discovery.

Index

Picture Credits

Cover photo: Art Resource, NY

AKG London, 30, 43 (bottom), 56 (both), 69, 73, 74, 75

American Museum of Natural History, 24, neg. no. 109353; 27 (both), neg. nos. 123868 and 123869; 44, neg. no. 315451; 50, neg. no. 335039, Singer; 70, neg. no. 323721, L. Boltin

Corbis-Bettmann, 17, 31, 67, 76

© E. R. Degginger, Science Source/Photo Researchers, 82

Field Museum of Natural History, Chicago, 48, neg. no. 76851; 55, neg. no. 102513; 68, neg. no. GEO-859083, John Weinstein

From *Prehistoric Man* by Bratislav Mazak, illustrated by Zdenek Burian. New York: The Hamlyn Publishing Group, 1980, 12

© Lowell Georgia/Corbis, 16

The Illustrated London News Picture Library, 9

Erich Lessing/Art Resource, NY, 15, 40

Mansell/Time Inc., 53, 58, 60, 79

© Tom McHugh, Science Source/Photo Researchers, 36

National Museums of Kenya, 46

Novosti, Science Source/Photo Researchers, 77

© John Reader, Science Source/Photo Researchers, 28, 32, 37, 38, 43 (top), 51

Stock Montage, Inc., 59, 63

University of Minnesota Libraries, 20, 33

UPI/Corbis-Bettmann, 10, 23, 25

About the Author

Patricia D. Netzley received a bachelor's degree in English from the University of California at Los Angeles (UCLA). After graduation she worked as an editor at the UCLA Medical Center, where she produced hundreds of medical articles, speeches, and pamphlets.

Netzley became a freelance writer in 1986. She is the author of several books for children and adults, including *The Assassination of President John F. Kennedy* (Macmillan/New Discovery Books, 1994), *Queen Victoria* (The Importance Of series, Lucent Books, 1996), *Alien Abductions* (Greenhaven Press, 1996), and *Butch Cassidy* (Mysterious Deaths series, Lucent Books, 1997). Her hobbies are weaving, knitting, and needlework. She and her husband, Raymond, live in southern California with their children, Matthew, Sarah, and Jacob.